GOOD FOOD FROM MICHIGAN

**A Collection of Recipes Featuring Michigan Grown
Fruits, Vegetables, and Sweeteners**

BY
LAURIE WOODY

River Run Press
Three Rivers, Michigan

*Additional copies of this book may be ordered through bookstores
or by sending $12.95 plus $3.50 for postage and handling to
Publishers Distribution Service
6893 Sullivan Road
Grawn, MI 49637
1- (800)-345-0096*

Published by River Run Press, Box 83, Three Rivers, Michigan 49093.

Publisher's Cataloging-in-Publication Data

Woody, Laurie –
     Good food from Michigan / by Laurie Woody
     p. cm.
     Includes index
     1. Cookery — Michigan. 2. Cookery, American.
I. Title.
TX715 1991 641.5 91-60234
ISBN 0-9629000-1-X

Manufactured in the United States of America

Cover Illustration by Jim Rutherford
Cover Design by Louan E. Lechler

ABOUT THIS BOOK

Do you ever have a hard time picking the best produce at the market? Or have you ever bought a lug of peaches because they looked so good, and then wondered how to use or store them once you got home? This book can help you out. Each chapter in the book has hints on selecting and storing the food featured in that chapter, as well as recipes using that food.

Several recipes in the book include microwave cooking instructions. The microwave recipes were tested in a 700 watt microwave oven. For the microwave recipes, always start with the shortest cooking time given and add more time if needed. Remember that you can always add more cooking time if needed, but you can't take it away once the food is overcooked! Make a note on the recipe when you find the right cooking time for your oven.

Each year Michigan grown foods are shipped to markets across the United States. In fact, agriculture is the 3rd largest industry in the state. This book features 24 different kinds of fruits, vegetables, and sweeteners grown commercially in Michigan. It was hard to decide which foods to include. There are many other foods which are grown and processed in Michigan which could have been included if space allowed.   Nationally, Michigan typically ranks 10th or higher in the production of each of the foods included in this book.

Many of the recipes and hints in the book have been shared by Michigan food processors, growers, grocery stores, restaurants and commodity groups. Other recipes were developed specifically for this book. Each recipe in the book has been personally tested by the author.

ABOUT THE AUTHOR

Laurie Woody graduated from Iowa State University with a degree in Home Economics. She worked as a corporate home economist for a large appliance manufacturer following graduation. Her work there involved recipe development, teaching cooking schools and answering questions from customers.

The first cookbook Laurie wrote was published by an agricultural company in the mid-west and used as a promotional item. Over 100,000 copies of that book have been distributed.

Laurie and her family moved to Michigan in 1986. Like many of the tourists, they were impressed by the wide variety of foods grown in Michigan. It was so interesting to see acres of green peppers and cucumbers growing along the highway, or to watch the asparagus sprout in early spring. Drives through the fruit orchards near Traverse City had to include a stop at farm markets along the way. Picking their own strawberries and apples at local farms is now an annual event for her family. This book was inspired by these visits to the beautiful growing areas of Michigan.

TABLE OF CONTENTS

ACKNOWLEDGEMENTS

A big thank you goes to the following groups and individuals who contributed recipes and helpful information to this book.

◊ American Celery Council
◊ American Spoon Foods
◊ Aunt Jane's Foods, Inc.
◊ Big Chief Sugar
  Monitor Sugar Company
◊ Gerry Buell
  Michigan Beekeepers
  Association
◊ Burnette Foods, Inc.
  Producers of Mother's Maid®
◊ Cherry Marketing Institute, Inc.
◊ Dodd's Sugar Shack
◊ Fenn Valley Vineyards
◊ Gerber Products Company
◊ Graceland Fruit Co-op
◊ Jerry Jollay
  Michigan Peach Sponsors
◊ Kellogg Company
◊ Livingston Farms
◊ Maynard Klamer
  Michigan Onion Committee
◊ Meijer, Inc.
◊ Barb Meyer
  Meyer Berry Farm
◊ MGB Marketing
◊ Michigan Agricultural
  Statistics Service
◊ Michigan Apple Committee
◊ Michigan Asparagus Advisory
  Board
◊ Michigan Celery Promotion
  Co-Operative, Inc.
◊ Michigan Department of
  Agriculture

◊ Michigan Onion Committee
◊ Michigan Plum Advisory
  Board
◊ Michigan State University
  Cooperative Extension
  Service
◊ Parmenter's Cider Mill, Inc.
◊ Peterson and Sons Winery
◊ David and Gale Phillips
  Wharfside
◊ Pioneer Sugar
  Michigan Sugar Company
◊ Randall Food Products
◊ St. Julian Wine Company, Inc.
◊ Martha Schaub
  Manitou Market and Bakery
◊ Schuler's, Inc.
◊ Marian Sheridan
  The Gourmet Cheesecake
  Club
◊ Ann Tennes
  The Country Mill
◊ The Michigan Bean
  Commision
◊ The Michigan Potato Industry
  Commission
◊ Thorn Apple Valley, Inc.
◊ Very Cherry Luncheon
  Sponsored by Michigan State
  University Cooperative
  Extension Service and The
  National Cherry Festival
◊ Welch's, Inc.

6

APPLES

MAJOR GROWING AREAS

Apple trees need a dormant period during the cold of winter to produce a good crop the next summer. When spring comes, the blossoms need to be protected against late frosts. Along the western side of the state, Lake Michigan moderates the weather to soften cold spring temperatures and delay the frost in the fall. These excellent growing conditions help Michigan to typically rank around second or third in apple production in the U.S.

Many different apple varieties are available in Michigan. The first summer apples are usually picked in mid-July and the fall varieties are picked through the end of October. Apples which will be used for salads, fruit cups or eaten fresh should be crisp, juicy and sweet. A good baking apple should retain it's shape and flavor during cooking.

The juice from the apple is available in two different forms. **Apple cider** is made from ground apples which are then pressed to extract the juice. Next the juice is strained to remove larger particles from the juice. The finer solid particles which are left give cider it's unique opaque look. After a few weeks in the refrigerator the natural sugars in the cider turn to alcohol and the flavor becomes more tangy. **Apple juice** starts out like cider, but finer solid particles are filtered out of the juice, leaving a bright, clear liquid. Apple juice is pasteurized and vacuum packed so the flavor stays fresh in an unopened container over a year without refrigeration.

HOW MUCH TO BUY ??? 3 medium apples are usually equal to 1 pound and should yield 2 to 3 cups of sliced apples. It generally takes 2 pounds of apples to make a 9-inch pie.

SELECTION: Look for a firm, crisp apple with color that is bright and appropriate for that variety (whether it be green, red, yellow or some-thing in between). The surface on the apple should be smooth and firm, with no bruises or blemishes. Brownish colored spots or streaks are likely due to "russeting". Generally, russeting is caused by weather conditions during the growing season. The russeting does not affect the

7

APPLES

flavor of the apple.

AVOID: Decay can spread rapidly from one apple to the next, so any decayed or badly bruised fruit should be discarded immediately.

STORAGE: Special storage techniques are used commercially to keep apples tasting fresh for months. At home, apples will store well for 2 to 3 weeks. Store apples in the coldest part of the refrigerator or crisper drawer. Apples should be wrapped in a perforated plastic bag. Apples stored at room temperature will ripen much more quickly than those in the refrigerator. Don't wash apples until just before using them.

Apples may be stored in a cool place like a garage for a short time during the fall harvest. When the temperatures start to drop at night, you may want to cover the fruit with plastic and /or blankets to insulate them from the cold.

Most peeled or cut apples will turn brown without special treatment. Cover apples with a water and lemon juice mixture, or use a commercial ascorbic acid treatment to prevent browning.

APPLE EXTRAS

* One of the apple varieties gaining popularity in Michigan is the Paulared. It was discovered on an orchard in Michigan.
* It takes 5 years of growth before apples can be harvested from the tree.
* A medium apple only has about 80 calories!

SPICY APPLE BREAD
Yield: 2 loaves

3/4 cup shortening
1 1/8 cups brown sugar, firmly packed
3 eggs
1 1/2 teaspoons vanilla
3 cups sifted all-purpose flour
1 1/2 teaspoons baking soda
1 1/2 teaspoons salt
1 1/2 teaspoons ground cinnamon
3/4 teaspoon ground nutmeg
1/2 teaspoon ground allspice
1/4 teaspoon ground cloves
1 1/2 cups grated apples
**3 tablespoons cider vinegar plus water to make 3/4 cup
   liquid**
3/4 cup chopped nuts

◊ Preheat oven to 350° F.
◊ Cream shortening and sugar. Add eggs one at a time, beating
   well after each addition. Add vanilla.
◊ Mix and sift together flour, soda, salt, cinnamon, nutmeg,
   allspice and cloves. Stir in flour mix alternating with grated
   apples and other liquid. Stir in nuts.
◊ Turn into 2 greased standard loaf pans (9 x 5) or 1 large
   greased loaf pan (11 1/2 x 4 1/2). Bake for 45 to 50 minutes
   (75 minutes for large loaf), or until toothpick inserted near
   center comes out clean.

Parmenter's Cider Mill, Inc.
Northville, Michigan

9

FRESH APPLE CAKE
Yield: 10-15 servings

3 eggs
1 3/4 cup sugar
2 cups all-purpose flour
1 teaspoon ground cinnamon
1 teaspoon baking soda
1/2 teaspoon salt
1 teaspoon vanilla
1 cup vegetable oil
4 apples, sliced thin
1 cup chopped walnuts
Powdered sugar

◊ Preheat oven to 350° F.
◊ Beat eggs to a lemon color. Add sugar, beating well. Add flour, cinnamon, baking soda and salt; mixing well. Add vanilla, oil, apples, and nuts . Pour batter into a greased 9 x 13-inch pan. Bake at 350° for 45 - 50 minutes, or until toothpick inserted near center comes out clean.
◊ When cake cools, sprinkle with powdered sugar.

Parmenter's Cider Mill, Inc.
Northville, Michigan

This is a fun recipe for fall. During football season, serve the cheese ball, crackers and apples slices at halftime!

APPLESAUCE CHEESE BALL
Yield: 1 cheese ball

1 (8 oz.) pkg. cream cheese
2/3 cup unsweetened applesauce
2 cups (8 oz.) shredded Cheddar cheese
1 1/2 cups (6 oz.) shredded Swiss cheese
Paprika
Apple slices
Crackers

◊ In large bowl, beat cream cheese until smooth. Slowly beat in applesauce, Cheddar cheese and Swiss cheese. Continue beating until blended evenly.
◊ Line a 3-cup bowl with plastic wrap. Pack cheese mixture into bowl, mounding top. Cover with plastic wrap and chill overnight.
◊ Before serving, remove plastic wrap. Trim away edge of cheese to round shape like an apple; press stem from fresh apple into top. Dust the cheese ball all over with paprika.
◊ Place cheese ball on serving platter. For best flavor, let stand at room temperature for 30 minutes before serving. Serve with apple slices and crackers.

11

PRETTY PINK APPLE SALAD
Yield: 8 servings

1 (8 oz.) can crushed pineapple, with syrup
2 eggs
1/2 cup sugar
1/4 cup lemon juice
1/2 cup raisins
2 1/2 cups diced, unpeeled apples
3/4 cup diced celery
1/8 teaspoon red food coloring
1/4 cup mayonnaise or salad dressing
2 cups whipped cream or frozen non-dairy topping, thawed

◊ Drain syrup from pineapple. Set pineapple aside. Combine pineapple syrup, eggs, sugar, and lemon juice. Stir until smooth. Cook in saucepan over moderate heat until slightly thickened, stirring frequently. Remove from heat and refrigerate until cooled.

◊ In a large bowl, combine reserved pineapple, raisins, apples and celery. Toss gently to mix. Set aside.

◊ Stir food coloring into cooled egg mixture. Fold in mayonnaise. Gently fold in whipped cream. Pour over apple mixture. Stir gently until blended. Fill a 6 to 8 cup mold and freeze at least 3 to 4 hours, or until firm.

◊ Unmold about 30 minutes before serving so that mixture will partially thaw. Do not serve frozen solid.

APPLESAUCE OATIES
Yield: 3 to 4 dozen cookies

3/4 cup margarine, softened
1 cup brown sugar, firmly packed
1 egg
1 teaspoon vanilla
1 cup all-purpose flour
1/2 teaspoon baking soda
1/2 teaspoon salt
3/4 teaspoon ground cinnamon
1/4 teaspoon ground cloves
2 jars (4.0-4.5 oz. each) GERBER APPLESAUCE
3 cups quick-cooking oats
1/2 cup raisins or chopped nuts

◊ Preheat oven to 350° F.
◊ Cream margarine well. Add sugar; cream until fluffy. Add egg and vanilla; beat well.
◊ Sift together flour, soda, salt, cinnamon and cloves. Add to creamed mixture alternately with applesauce. Stir in oats and raisins or nuts.
◊ Drop by teaspoonfuls onto lightly greased cookie sheet. Bake at 350° for 12 - 15 minutes, or until lightly browned. Remove from cookie sheet and cool on wire racks.

Gerber Products Company
Fremont, Michigan

13

APPLES

APPLE CRANBERRY SAUCE
Yield: 1 1/2 quarts sauce

1 (16 oz.) bag cranberries (about 4 cups)*
4 apples, cored and unpeeled
1 orange, peeled
2 cups sugar
1 (3 oz.) pkg. orange flavored gelatin
1 1/2 cups boiling water

◊ Process cranberries, apples and orange in food grinder or food processor until finely chopped. Place in large bowl. Mix the sugar into the fruit. Set aside.
◊ Dissolve gelatin in boiling water and refrigerate until partially set.
◊ Mix gelatin with chopped fruit. Return to refrigerator until set.
◊ HINT: This may be made days ahead. It stores well in the refrigerator to use throughout the holidays.

* Many cranberries are packaged in 12 oz. bags. You may need to use 1 1/3 bags to get 4 cups of berries. Cranberries do freeze well and the partial bag may be used in the recipe for Festive Fall Cobbler.

Ann Tennes
The Country Mill
Charlotte, Michigan

*When I tested this recipe, my husband took two bites and said, "I definitely want you to make this again. It is **good**!"*

COUNTRY APPLE DESSERT
Yield: 12 servings

1 (18.5 oz.) pkg. yellow cake mix
2 eggs
1/3 cup margarine, softened
1 (20 oz.) can Mother's Maid Apple Pie Filling
1/2 cup brown sugar, firmly packed
1/2 cup chopped nuts
1 teaspoon ground cinnamon
1 cup dairy sour cream
1 teaspoon vanilla

◊ Preheat oven to 350° F.
◊ In a large bowl, combine cake mix, 1 egg and margarine at low speed until crumbly. Press in ungreased 9x13-inch pan. Spoon pie filling over crust. Combine brown sugar, nuts and cinnamon. Sprinkle over apples.
◊ In a small bowl, blend sour cream, 1 egg and vanilla. Pour over sugar mixture. Bake at 350° for 40 to 50 minutes, or until topping is golden around the edges. Serve warm or cool. Refrigerate leftovers.

Burnette Foods Inc.
Producers of Mother's Maid®
Elk Rapids, Michigan

APPLE PIE COFFEE CAKE
Yield: 6 to 8 servings

1 1/4 cups all-purpose flour
1/4 teaspoon salt
2 tablespoons brown sugar
1 teaspoon baking powder
1/2 cup butter or margarine
1 egg
2 tablespoons cold coffee (or water)
2 medium apples
1/2 cup sugar
1 tablespoon all-purpose flour
1 teaspoon ground cinnamon
1/8 teaspoon ground ginger
1/8 teaspoon ground cloves
1/8 teaspoon ground nutmeg

◊ Preheat oven to 350° F.
◊ In a medium bowl, combine 1 1/4 cups flour, salt, brown sugar and baking powder. Cut in butter until size of small peas. Combine egg and coffee. Stir into flour mixture until just blended. Press into bottom and 1 inch up sides of lightly greased 9-inch round baking pan.
◊ Core, peel and thinly slice each apple. Combine sugar, 1 tablespoon flour, cinnamon, ginger, cloves and nutmeg in a medium bowl. Stir apples into sugar mixture. Sprinkle apples and sugar over crust. Bake at 350° for 45 to 50 minutes, or until apples are tender. Serve warm.

16

CARAMEL CRUNCH APPLE PIE
Yield: 1, 9-inch pie

28 vanilla dairy caramels
2 tablespoons water
4 cups peeled, sliced Michigan apples
1 unbaked 9-inch pie shell
3/4 cup all-purpose flour
1/3 cup sugar
1/2 teaspoon ground cinnamon
1/3 cup butter or margarine
1/2 cup chopped walnuts

◊ Preheat oven to 375° F.
◊ Melt caramels with water in top of double boiler, stirring occasionally until mixture is smooth.
◊ Layer apples and caramel sauce in pie shell.
◊ Combine flour, sugar and cinnamon. Cut in butter or margarine until mixture is crumbly; stir in walnuts. Sprinkle over top of pie.
◊ Bake at 375° for 50 to 60 minutes, or until apples are tender.

Michigan Apple Committee
DeWitt, Michigan

CINNAMON APPLE SALAD
Yield: 4 servings

1/4 cup "red hots" cinnamon candies
1 cup boiling water, divided
1 (3 oz.) pkg. red gelatin
1 cup cold apple cider
2 cups Michigan McIntosh apples, peeled and chopped
1/4 cup nuts, chopped

◊ Dissolve cinnamon candies in 1/2 cup boiling water.
◊ In medium bowl, add 1/2 cup boiling water to gelatin and stir
  until dissolved. Stir in apple cider and cinnamon-candy-water
  mixture.
◊ Refrigerate until partially set.
◊ Add chopped apples and nuts. Refrigerate until firm.

◊ NOTE: This salad is excellent with hot and spicy food such as
  chili.

Michigan Apple Committee
DeWitt, Michigan

Suggested Menu

Chili Bean Soup
Cinnamon Apple Salad
Honey Oatmeal Bread
Peaches and Cream Cheesecake

SPICED CIDER
Yield: 1 gallon

1 gallon apple cider
4 sticks cinnamon
1/2 teaspoon whole allspice
1/2 teaspoon whole cloves

◊ Bring cider to a boil. Add cinnamon sticks, allspice, and
cloves. Let stand 4 hours.
◊ Strain cider to remove spices. Refrigerate until ready to serve.
◊ Serve warm or cold.

Ann Tennes
The Country Mill
Charlotte, Michigan

FINGER JUICE
Yield: 12 blocks

3 (4.2 fl. oz. each) bottles GERBER APPLE or GERBER
APPLE-CHERRY JUICE
2 (1/4 oz. each) envelopes unflavored gelatin

◊ MICROWAVE DIRECTIONS: In a 1-quart square casserole,
sprinkle unflavored gelatin over juice; let stand 3 minutes.
Microwave at high power 1 minute; stir thoroughly. Then
microwave at high power 2 minutes. Remove from microwave
and stir until gelatin is completely dissolved. Chill until firm,
about 3 hours. Cut into 1-inch squares.
◊ CONVENTIONAL DIRECTIONS: In medium saucepan,
sprinkle unflavored gelatin over juice; let stand 1 minute. Stir
over low heat until gelatin is completely dissolved, about 5
minutes. Pour into 1-quart square casserole and chill as
above. Cut into 1-inch squares.

Gerber Products Company
Fremont, Michigan

APPLE DANISH BARS
Yield: 12 to 15 servings

2 1/2 cups all-purpose flour
1/2 teaspoon salt
1 cup (2 sticks) butter or margarine
1 egg, separated
Milk (up to 2/3 cup)
1 cup crisped rice cereal
7 medium apples, peeled, cored and sliced
1 teaspoon ground cinnamon
1 cup brown sugar, firmly packed
1 tablespoon lemon juice
1 tablespoon butter or margarine
1 1/2 cups powdered sugar
2 tablespoons milk

◊ Preheat oven to 375° F.
◊ In a large mixing bowl, stir together flour and salt. Cut in 1 cup
  butter until mixture resembles coarse crumbs.
◊ Combine egg yolk and enough milk to make 2/3 cup liquid. Set
  aside egg white. Add yolk-milk mixture to flour mixture and stir
  until combined. Divide dough in half. Roll 1/2 of dough out on
  lightly floured surface into a 9 x 13-inch rectangle. Place dough
  in lightly greased 9 x 13-inch pan.
◊ Sprinkle crisped rice cereal over dough in pan.
◊ In a medium bowl, combine apples, cinnamon, brown sugar
  and lemon juice. Toss together until mixed. Arrange apples
  over cereal and dough.
◊ On a lightly floured surface, roll remaining dough into a 9 x 13-
  inch rectangle. Place on top of apple layer in pan. Beat egg
  white until frothy. Brush egg white over top crust. Bake at
  375° for 30 to 35 minutes, or until apples are tender.
◊ For frosting, cream 1 tablespoon butter in a small bowl. Add
  powdered sugar and milk and beat until smooth. Add extra
  sugar or milk as needed. Frost apple bars while warm.

ASPARAGUS

The appearance of fresh asparagus in late April is a sure sign of spring. Unfortunately for those of us who love fresh asparagus, it is a short season with harvest completed in early June. It is possible to enjoy canned or frozen asparagus throughout the year, but the

MAJOR GROWING AREAS

taste of garden fresh asparagus that has been lightly seasoned and cooked to the crisp-tender stage is a real treat.

It is not until the plant's third growing season that the first stalk of asparagus can be harvested. After 6 to 8 years, asparagus reaches its prime and can yield as much 1 ton per acre. Asparagus is low in calories (only about 4 per spear) and high in nutrients!

Michigan ranks 3rd in asparagus production in the United States. Most of the asparagus crop is processed (canned or frozen). Along the Lake Michigan shoreline, the moderate temperatures and loamy sand in the soil make for excellent asparagus production. The Michigan Asparagus Advisory Board notes that in Michigan, asparagus is hand-snapped above the ground as it is harvested. This means less waste for con-sumers because only about 1/4-inch of the stalk end needs to be discarded before cooking.

HOW MUCH TO BUY??? 1 pound snapped asparagus yields approxi-mately 2 cups cut-up asparagus.

SELECTION: Look for tender, bright green stalks with closed, compact tips and a firm, fresh appearance. Select stalks with the same diameter so they will cook evenly. Stalk size (thin vs. fat) does not affect tender-ness. It is a matter of personal preference.

AVOID: Avoid asparagus with open tips which may have been picked past it's prime. Do not choose asparagus with tips that are soggy or decayed or with other signs of deterioration.

21

ASPARAGUS

STORAGE: Wash the asparagus thoroughly. Place it in a moisture proof wrapping. Store asparagus in the crisper drawer of the refrigerator. Asparagus may also be stored upright in water. To do this, trim the stalk end about 1/4-inch and stand upright in a few inches of cold water, covering tops with plastic. Use fresh asparagus within 2-3 days for best quality. Don't cut asparagus into pieces until just before you are ready to cook the asparagus.

CREAM OF ASPARAGUS SOUP
Yield: 6 servings

1 pound asparagus pieces, fresh, frozen or canned
1 medium onion, chopped
1/4 cup butter or margarine
1/4 cup all-purpose flour
1/2 teaspoon salt
1/4 teaspoon ground nutmeg (optional)
Milk (up to 1 quart)
Shredded cheese or croutons

◊ Cook fresh or frozen asparagus in a small amount of water until tender. Drain asparagus, reserving liquid.
◊ Cook onion in butter until soft. Stir in flour, salt and nutmeg; cook and stir until pasty. Add enough milk to reserved asparagus liquid to make one quart. Add to flour mixture, cooking and stirring until slightly thickened.
◊ If desired, twirl 3/4 of the asparagus in blender. Add asparagus to milk mixture and heat through.
◊ Garnish with shredded cheese or croutons.

Michigan Asparagus Advisory Board
Lansing, Michigan

ASPARAGUS AND CHICKEN STIR-FRY
Yield: 2 servings

1 teaspoon sesame seeds
1 boneless chicken breast, sliced into thin strips
1/2 pound asparagus spears (about 12 spears), cleaned and
  diagonally sliced
3 green onions, sliced
1 tablespoon soy sauce
2 teaspoons sugar
Salt
Pepper
Hot, cooked rice

◊ Preheat a skillet or wok; add sesame seeds. Stir frequently
  and continue cooking until sesame seeds are lightly toasted.
◊ Add the chicken; stir-fry until chicken is cooked and no longer
  pink, stirring often. Push chicken to side of pan.
◊ Add asparagus and green onion to skillet. Stir-fry until vegetables are crisp-tender. Stir together vegetables and chicken.
◊ Stir soy sauce and sugar into mixture in skillet.   Season with
  salt and pepper, as desired. Serve immediately with hot,
  cooked rice.

ALMOND ASPARAGUS
Yield: 4 servings

2 cups fresh asparagus
2 tablespoons margarine
1 tablespoon lemon juice
1/2 cup blanched, slivered, toasted almonds
Salt
Pepper

◊ Wash asparagus; cut into one-inch diagonal slices.
◊ Heat margarine in skillet, then add asparagus and sauté three
   to four minutes.
◊ Cover skillet and steam about two minutes or until tender-crisp.
◊ Toss asparagus with lemon juice and almonds; salt and pepper
   to taste.

Meijer, Inc.
Grand Rapids, Michigan

LAYERED ASPARAGUS SUPREME
Yield: 4 servings

1 (10 oz.) pkg. frozen asparagus, cooked and drained
2 hard cooked eggs, sliced
1 (10 3/4 oz.) cream of celery soup
1/3 cup slivered almonds
1/2 cup (2 oz.) grated Cheddar cheese

◊ Preheat oven to 350° F.
◊ Place cooked and drained asparagus in bottom of a lightly
   greased 1 1/2 or 2-quart casserole.
◊ Arrange sliced eggs over asparagus.
◊ Spoon soup over egg layer.
◊ Sprinkle almonds over soup.
◊ Sprinkle Cheddar cheese over almonds. Bake at 350° for 20 to
   25 minutes, or until cheese is melted and mixture is heated
   through.

24

ASPARAGUS AND CHEESE PUFF
Yield: 8 servings

1 (10 oz.) pkg. frozen asparagus
1 (10 3/4 oz.) can cream of asparagus soup
1 soup can milk (about 1 1/3 cups)
1/4 cup all-purpose flour
2 teaspoons Dijon mustard
1/4 teaspoon black pepper
2 cups (8 oz.) shredded Cheddar cheese
4 eggs, yolks and whites separated

◊ Preheat oven to 350° F.
◊ Cook asparagus according to package directions. Cool, drain and set aside.
◊ Mix soup, milk, flour, mustard and pepper in a 3-quart sauce-pan until blended. Cook over medium-high heat until almost boiling, stirring frequently. (Mixture may also be microwaved. Using a microwave safe, 3-quart casserole, cook on high power for 4 to 5 minutes, or until almost boiling. Stir each minute during cooking time.)
◊ Remove from heat. Add cheese and stir until melted. Slice cooked, cooled asparagus into 1/4-inch thick pieces. Stir asparagus and egg yolks into cheese and soup mixture.
◊ Beat egg whites in a medium-size bowl with electric mixer until stiff peaks form. Fold into asparagus mixture. Pour into lightly greased 2 or 3-quart shallow casserole dish. Bake at 350° for 50 minutes, or until top is golden and puffy and knife inserted near center comes out clean. Let stand 5 minutes before serving.

ASPARAGUS BRUNCH BUNDLES
Yield: 4 servings

1 sheet puff pastry
1 (10 oz.) box frozen asparagus spears or 1 lb. fresh aspara-
  gus spears, cooked and cooled
Thinly sliced ham

◊ Preheat oven to 400° F.
◊ Cut puff pastry into strips 1 inch wide (about 9 strips).
◊ Place 2 or 3 asparagus spears on ham slice. Roll up as for
  jelly roll. Spiral puff pastry around ham roll.
◊ Place on ungreased baking sheet. Bake at 400° for about 15
  to 20 minutes, or until pastry is puffed and browned. Serve at
  once.

Michigan Asparagus Advisory Board
Lansing, Michigan

Suggested Menu

Onion Soup
Asparagus Brunch Bundles
Gingered Fruit Cup
Pudding Surprise

BLUEBERRIES

MAJOR GROWING AREAS

Of all the fruits available throughout the year, blueberries are one of the most convenient to use. After blueberries are washed, they are ready to be enjoyed. There is no need for peeling, pitting, or seeding. Fresh blueberries are available during July, August and usually into September. During the other months, frozen and canned blueberries are readily available.

Blueberries require special growing conditions. The soil must be acidic and regular watering is important. The cold temperatures over the winter in Michigan give the bushes a dormant period important for a good blueberry crop.

According to the Michigan Blueberry Growers Association, about 95% of the world's commercial blueberries are grown in North America. Michigan is this nation's biggest producer of commercially grown blueberries. Look for blueberries at the market, or pick your own at one of the many "U-pick" farms in the state! Enjoy blueberries in breads, muffins, desserts, salads or pies.

HOW MUCH TO BUY??? One pound equals 2 to 2 1/2 cups of blueberries. There are usually 3 to 4 servings in a pint of blueberries.

SELECTION: Look for blueberries with a dark blue color and a silvery bloom (this is the natural protective wax on the blueberry). Choose firm, plump berries which are uniform in size.

AVOID: Set aside blueberries which are moldy, bruised or smashed. Decay will spread quickly from one blueberry to the next, so discard any berries which show signs of decay.

STORAGE: Do not wash blueberries until just before using them. Blueberries should be covered with plastic wrap and stored in the crisper section of the refrigerator. Blueberries will store well in the refrigerator for one to two weeks.

Blueberries may be frozen in a single layer on a cookie sheet. Transfer the berries to a freezer storage bag once they are frozen. Pour frozen berries from the freezer bag as needed. Blueberries may also be frozen in a syrup pack.

BLUEBERRY FOOL
Yield: 4 servings

2 cups fresh or frozen blueberries
1/2 cup sugar
2 tablespoons water
1/2 teaspoon lemon juice
1/4 teaspoon ground nutmeg
1 cup whipping cream

◊ In a medium saucepan, combine blueberries, sugar and water. Cook over low heat, stirring often, until berries are tender. Lightly mash berries with fork. Process mixture in a blender or food processor until puréed. Cover and refrigerate mixture several hours.
◊ Just before serving, whip cream until peaks form. Fold chilled blueberry mixture into whipped cream. Spoon into serving bowls. If desired, garnish with additional blueberries.

No collection of blueberry recipes would be complete without a recipe for blueberry muffins.

BLUEBERRY MUFFINS
Yield: 18 muffins

2 cups all-purpose flour
2 teaspoons baking powder
1 teaspoon ground cinnamon
1/4 teaspoon salt
2 eggs
1 cup milk
3/4 cup sugar
1/2 cup vegetable oil
1 cup fresh or frozen North American blueberries, thawed if necessary

◊ Preheat oven to 400° F.
◊ Combine flour, baking powder, cinnamon and salt; mix well. Beat eggs lightly; stir in milk, sugar and oil. Quickly stir egg mixture into dry ingredients; carefully stir in blueberries. Spoon into greased muffin cups; bake at 400° for 15 to 17 minutes, or until top springs back when lightly touched.

MGB Marketing/ Michigan Blueberry Growers Association
Grand Junction, Michigan

The hint of orange flavor in this pie gives it a special taste. Blueberry lovers will want to add this to their recipe collection!

LATTICE-TOPPED BLUEBERRY PIE
Yield: 1, 9-inch pie

3/4 cup sugar
1/4 cup all-purpose flour
1 teaspoon ground cinnamon
1 teaspoon grated orange peel
4 cups fresh or frozen blueberries, thawed if necessary
Pastry for 2 crust (9-inch) pie
2 tablespoons orange juice
1 tablespoon butter or margarine

◊ Preheat oven to 425° F.
◊ Combine sugar, flour, cinnamon and orange peel; lightly toss with blueberries.   Place in pastry-lined pie plate. Sprinkle with orange juice; dot top with butter. Roll out remaining pastry; cut into 1/2-inch strips. Arrange in lattice pattern on top of pie. Moisten edge of lower crust; fold over lattice ends, seal and flute. Bake at 425° for 10 minutes; lower to 350° F and bake 35 to 40 minutes or until crust is golden brown and filling begins to bubble.

◊ QUICK METHOD DIRECTIONS: Prepare pie in microwave-safe pie plate. Cook in microwave on high power for 10 minutes; bake at 425° F 10 minutes or until crust is golden brown and filling begins to bubble.

MGB Marketing/ Michigan Blueberry Growers Association
Grand Junction

BLUEBERRY LOAVES
Yield: 2 loaves

2 (1/4 oz. each) pkgs. active dry yeast
1/2 cup lukewarm water
1 cup warm milk
1/4 cup butter or margarine, softened
1/4 cup sugar
1/2 teaspoon salt
4 1/2 to 5 cups all-purpose flour
1 egg
1 cup fresh blueberries
1/3 cup sugar
3 teaspoons ground cinnamon
1/2 teaspoon ground nutmeg

◊ Combine yeast and lukewarm water in large bowl. Let stand about 5 minutes, or until yeast is soft.
◊ Stir together milk and butter until butter is melted. Add milk mixture, 1/4 cup sugar and salt to softened yeast. Add 3 cups of the flour. Mix to blend, then beat on low speed until smooth and elastic. Beat in egg.
◊ Stir in 1 more cup flour to make a soft dough. Turn out onto lightly floured board. Knead until dough is smooth and elastic, working in remaining 1/2 to 1 cup flour as needed.
◊ Transfer dough to lightly greased bowl. Cover and let rise until doubled (about 45 - 60 minutes).
◊ Punch down dough. Divide dough into 2 parts. Roll 1 part dough into 18 x 9-inch rectangle. Lightly chop blueberries. Sprinkle 1/2 blueberries over dough. Mix together 1/3 cup sugar, cinnamon and nutmeg. Sprinkle 1/2 sugar mixture over dough. Starting at short side, tightly roll up dough to form loaf. Press edge to seal and fold ends under. Place in greased loaf pan. Repeat with remaining dough and filling.
◊ Let rise until double (about 30 to 45 minutes). Bake in **pre-heated 375° F oven** for 35 to 45 minutes, or until each loaf sounds hollow when tapped.

SOUR CREAM BLUEBERRY PIE
Yield: 1, 9-inch pie

3 cups blueberries
1 unbaked 9-inch pie shell
1 1/4 cup sugar
1/2 cup all-purpose flour
Dash salt
1 (8 oz.) carton dairy sour cream (1 cup)

◊ Preheat oven to 450° F.
◊ Spread blueberries in unbaked pie shell. In medium bowl, stir
together sugar, flour and salt. Stir in sour cream, mixing well.
◊ Spoon sour cream mixture over blueberries. Spread mixture
evenly over berries and to edge of shell.
◊ Bake at 450° for 10 minutes.
◊ Reduce heat to 350° F and bake an additional 40 to 50 minutes, or until top is firm and lightly browned. Cool and serve at
room temperature.

Suggested Menu

Ham and Bean Casserole
Cornmeal Muffins
Make Ahead Michigan Salad
Sour Cream Blueberry Pie

BLUEBERRY COFFEE CAKE
Yield: 12 servings

1 1/2 cups sugar
2/3 cup shortening
2 eggs, well beaten
3 1/3 cup all-purpose flour, divided
3 teaspoons baking powder
1/2 teaspoon salt
2/3 cup buttermilk
2 cups blueberries
1 tablespoon sugar
1/2 teaspoon ground cinnamon

◊ Preheat oven to 375° F.
◊ In a large bowl, cream together 1 1/2 cups sugar and shortening. Add eggs and continue beating until fluffy.
◊ Sift together 3 cups flour, baking powder and salt. Add flour mixture to creamed mixture alternately with buttermilk.
◊ Toss remaining 1/3 cup flour with blueberries. Fold into cake batter. Spread in a greased 9 x 13-inch pan. Sprinkle 1 tablespoon sugar and cinnamon over top of cake.
◊ Bake at 375° for 35 to 40 minutes, or until a toothpick inserted in center comes out clean.

LEMON GLAZED BLUEBERRY TURNOVERS
Yield: 12 turnovers

1 (8 oz.) pkg. cream cheese, softened
1 cup (2 sticks) butter or margarine
1 tablespoon lemon juice
1 teaspoon grated lemon peel
2 cups all-purpose flour
1/2 (21 oz.) can blueberry pie filling
1/2 cup powdered sugar
2 teaspoons lemon juice

◊ Beat together cream cheese, butter, 1 tablespoon lemon juice, and lemon peel. Gradually stir in flour to form soft dough. Refrigerate at least 30 minutes, or until chilled.
◊ Preheat oven to 350° F.
◊ On a lightly floured surface, roll dough into a 12x16-inch rectangle, using additional flour as needed to prevent sticking.
◊ Cut dough into 12 squares. Spoon generous tablespoon pie filling on to center of one square. Fold one corner of the square diagonally to other corner, forming a triangle. Pinch the edges together to seal in pie filling. Place on greased cookie sheet. Repeat with remaining squares of dough.
◊ Bake at 350° for 30 to 35 minutes, or until golden. Cool.
◊ Stir together powdered sugar and lemon juice to make a glaze. Drizzle over turnovers.

CANTALOUPE

The "Michigan Melons Sold Here" signs spread from Michigan to Indiana and over into Ohio in August. The sweet flavor of Michigan grown cantaloupes and watermelons are definitely worth advertising! Look for Michigan cantaloupe during the months of August and September.

MAJOR GROWING AREAS

Even though they are full of flavor, cantaloupes are low in calories and rich in Vitamins A and C. Melons should be picked when they are mature, but may need a few days to fully ripen.

HOW MUCH TO BUY??? 1 medium cantaloupe generally serves 2 people.

SELECTION: Check the stem end of the melon. On a mature cantaloupe, the stem should be gone and a smooth indentation should remain. The netting on the fruit should be yellow to light green or gray and should be cord-like and prominent. A mature cantaloupe may need time to fully ripen. A ripe cantaloupe will yield to slight pressure on the stem end of the melon and have a pleasant "cantaloupe" odor.

AVOID: Try to avoid overripe cantaloupe which has a pronounced yellow color and softness to the rind. If the stem is still there, or if the stem was torn from the fruit, the melon was probably picked before it was mature. Discard fruit with large bruised areas and those with mold near the stem scar (this indicates decay).

STORAGE: Even if a cantaloupe was picked when fully mature, it may need time to ripen for best flavor. A ripe cantaloupe has a yellow cast to the rind and has a pleasant "cantaloupe" smell when held near the nose. To ripen, store cantaloupe at room temperature for a 2 to 4 days, or until it is ripe. Fully ripened cantaloupe should be refrigerated and will keep for up to a week. Cut melons should be covered with plastic wrap before refrigerating.

35

LIME-POPPY SEED DRESSING FOR MELON SALADS
Yield: 1 1/2 cups dressing

1 (6 oz.) can limeade concentrate
3/4 cup vegetable oil
1 tablespoon vinegar
1 teaspoon poppy seed

◊ Place limeade concentrate, vegetable oil and vinegar in blender. Process until smooth.
◊ Stir in poppy seed.
◊ HINT: This dresssing may be served over any fresh fruit salad, but it is especially good with melon salads. You may want to try this idea - combine cut-up watermelon, cantaloupe, and honeydew melons. Drizzle dressing over fruit as desired.
◊ HINT: Extra dressing may be frozen and used later.

SUMMER FRUIT SALAD
Yield: 6 to 8 servings

1 (20 oz.) can pineapple chunks, with juice
2 tablespoons cornstarch
1/4 cup sugar
1 cantaloupe, peeled and diced
1 cup seedless green grapes

◊ Drain juice from pineapple chunks and set aside.   Cut grapes in half. Add grapes and melon to pineapple chunks.
◊ Add cornstarch and sugar to reserved pineapple juice. Heat juice mixture until it is clear and thickened. Cool slightly. Pour thickened juice over fruit. Chill until served.

MELON BOATS
Yield: 4 servings

1 cantaloupe
1 pint sherbet
Fresh blueberries

◊ Cut cantaloupe in half lengthwise. Remove seeds. Cut each half in half again, forming 4 melon "boats".
◊ Place each boat on a serving plate. Place a scoop of sherbet in the center of melon boat. Sprinkle fresh blueberries over melon and sherbet. Serve immediately.

BANANA-CANTALOUPE DELIGHT
Yield: 6 servings

1 cup plain low-fat yogurt
1 tablespoon orange juice concentrate
1 tablespoon brown sugar
1 teaspoon vanilla flavoring
1/4 teaspoon ground nutmeg
1 cantaloupe
1 kiwi fruit
2 bananas

◊ Combine yogurt, orange juice concentrate, brown sugar, vanilla and nutmeg. Whisk until smooth. Set aside.
◊ Cut cantaloupe in half lengthwise. Remove seeds. Either remove peel and cut melon into bite-size pieces or use melon baller to cut melon into melon balls. Peel and thinly slice kiwi and bananas. Combine cantaloupe, kiwi and bananas.
◊ Divide into 6 dessert dishes. Spoon yogurt topping over fruit. Serve immediately.

37

This recipes doubles as a salad or appetizer. When served as kebabs, the recipe may be made ahead and put on wooden picks just before serving.

FRUIT KEBABS
Yield: 4 to 6 servings

**1/2 cantaloupe
1 cup pineapple chunks (fresh or canned pineapple may be used)
1 cup small, red, seedless grapes
1 kiwi fruit, peeled and sliced
1/4 cup pineapple juice
1 tablespoon honey
1/2 teaspoon vanilla**

◊ Remove seeds from 1/2 melon and scoop the melon into balls. If desired, melon shell may be saved for serving dish.
◊ Toss the melon balls, pineapple chunks, grapes and kiwi slices together in a medium bowl.
◊ In a small bowl, whisk together the pineapple juice, honey and vanilla. Pour over fruit, cover and refrigerate for 1 to 2 hours.
◊ When ready to serve either make fruit kebabs by threading the fruit on wooden picks or serve fruit mixture in hollow melon shell.
◊ NOTE: Grape juice may be substituted for pineapple juice.

CARROTS

The carrot is a versatile and nutritious vegetable. Rich in Vitamin A, the carrot is low in calories. Carrots are equally good served raw or cooked, in salads, soups, casseroles, side dishes or even as carrot cake!

MAJOR GROWING AREAS

With over 95,000 tons of carrots produced in the state each year, Michigan typically ranks around 4th in carrot production in the United States. Look for Michigan grown carrots from July through November. Carrots with green tops still on the carrots are the freshest, but carrots with green tops still attached are available only a few weeks of the year.

HOW MUCH TO BUY??? One pound usually serves 3 people and will yield 2 1/2 cups of shredded carrots.

SELECTION: Carrots should be firm, smooth, well-formed and a deep orange color. Generally, carrots with a small diameter will be more tender and sweet. The freshest carrots are those with the green tops still attached. The tops should be removed before storing carrots.

AVOID: Large green "sunburned" areas at the top of the carrot must be discarded and should be avoided. Carrots which show signs of decay, are wilted, split or have major blemishes should not be chosen.

STORAGE: The green tops on fresh carrots will draw moisture from the carrots, so cut off the green tops. Refrigerate carrots in plastic bags. Carrots will store well for a few months in the crisper section of the refrigerator.

Carrots freeze well, but should be blanched before freezing. When canning carrots, a pressure canner must always be used.

39

CHICKEN AND CARROT CASSEROLE
Yield: 4 servings

2 cups seasoned croutons
1/2 cup water
1/4 cup butter or margarine, melted
1 egg
3/4 cup milk
1 cup cubed, cooked chicken
1/4 cup chopped celery
1/4 cup chopped onion
3/4 cup shredded carrots
1 (10 3/4 oz.) can cream of mushroom soup

◊ Preheat oven to 350° F.
◊ In medium mixing bowl, stir together croutons, water and
   butter. Stir together egg and milk; pour over crouton mixture.
   Stir until blended. Add chicken, celery, onion and carrots. Stir
   until blended. Pour mixture into a lightly greased 9x9-inch
   baking dish.
◊ Spoon cream of mushroom soup over casserole. Bake in 350°
   oven for 35 to 45 minutes, or until bubbling. Serve warm.

CARROTS AU GRATIN
Yield: 8 servings

5 tablespoons margarine or butter
1 1/2 cups Kellogg's Corn Flakes ® cereal, crushed to 3/4
  cup
1/3 cup chopped onion
3 tablespoons all-purpose flour
1 teaspoon salt
1/8 teaspoon pepper
1 1/2 cups milk
1 cup shredded American cheese
4 cups sliced carrots, cooked and drained (about 1 1/2 lbs.)
1 tablespoon dried parsley flakes

◊ Melt 2 tablespoons margarine. Combine with crushed
  Kellogg's Corn Flakes cereal; set aside for topping.
◊ Melt remaining 3 tablespoons margarine in large saucepan
  over low heat. Add onion. Cook, stirring frequently, until onion
  is softened but not browned. Stir in flour, salt and pepper. Add
  milk gradually, stirring until smooth. Increase heat to medium
  and cook until bubbly and thickened, stirring constantly. Add
  cheese, stirring until melted. Remove from heat. Stir in carrots
  and parsley flakes. Spread mixture in greased 10x6x2-inch (1
  1/2-quart) glass baking dish. Sprinkle cereal mixture evenly
  over top.
◊ Bake at 350° F about 20 minutes or until thoroughly heated
  and bubbly. Remove from oven. Let stand about 5 minutes
  before serving.

Kellogg Company
Battle Creek, Michigan

SUNRISE MUFFINS
Yield: 18 muffins

2 cups all-purpose flour
1 1/4 cups sugar
2 teaspoons ground cinnamon
2 teaspoons baking soda
2 cups shredded carrots
1/2 cup raisins
1 cup dry roasted peanuts, chopped
1 apple, peeled and shredded
2 eggs
3/4 cup vegetable oil
2 teaspoons vanilla

◊ Preheat oven to 375° F.
◊ Sift together flour, sugar, cinnamon and baking soda. Combine carrots, raisins, peanuts and apple. Stir into flour mixture.
◊ In small bowl, beat together eggs, oil and vanilla. Stir into flour mixture until batter is just combined.
◊ Spoon into well-greased muffin tins, filling to the top.
◊ Bake muffins at 375° degrees for 20 minutes, or until top springs back when lightly pressed with finger.

This soup really is delicious!

CARROT SOUP
Yield: 4 servings

6 carrots, peeled and thinly sliced
1 medium onion, chopped
1 clove garlic, minced
2 (13 3/4 oz. each) cans chicken broth or 3 1/2 cups chicken
  stock
3 tablespoons uncooked rice
1/2 teaspoon basil leaves
1 teaspoon salt
1/4 teaspoon pepper
1 cup half and half cream
Parsley (for garnish)

◊ Combine carrots, onion, garlic, chicken broth, rice, basil, salt
  and pepper in medium saucepan. Cook over medium heat for
  30 minutes, or until vegetables are tender.
◊ Using about 1/3 of the vegetable mixture at a time, purée in a
  food processor or blender until smooth.
◊ Return to saucepan. Add half and half to puréed vegetables.
  Warm mixture over low heat, being careful to avoid boiling
  mixture. Stir frequently. Serve warm and garnish with a sprig
  of parsley.
◊ HINT: Soup may also be refrigerated and served cold.

My mother-in-law shared this carrot recipe. It stores well in the refrigerator and is a favorite at potluck dinners.

PICKLED CARROTS
Yield: 8 servings

2 pounds carrots
1 green pepper
1 medium onion
1 (10 3/4 oz.) can condensed tomato soup
1/2 cup vegetable oil
3/4 cup sugar
3/4 cup vinegar
1 teaspoon dry mustard
1 teaspoon Worcestershire sauce
1/2 teaspoon ground black pepper

◊ Clean and slice carrots. In a medium saucepan, cover carrots with water and boil until carrots are crisp-tender. Rinse with cold water to stop cooking. Drain.
◊ Chop green pepper and onion. Place in a large bowl. Stir in cooked carrots.
◊ In medium bowl, combine soup, vegetable oil, sugar, vinegar, dry mustard, Worcestershire sauce and pepper. Whisk until smooth. Pour over prepared vegetables.
◊ Refrigerate several hours, or overnight, to allow flavors to blend.

CELERY

Celery is at the top of every dieter's list of good foods to eat. With less than 10 calories in one large stalk, it's easy to see why. Stir-fries, stuffings, and many soups just wouldn't be the same without celery to add that extra flavor. Leave cut-up celery sticks in a plastic bag in the refrigerator for handy snacks. Or, try stuffing stalks of celery with cheese spread, peanut butter, or cream cheese.

MAJOR GROWING AREAS

Commercial production of celery in this country began in Kalamazoo where it was introduced by Dutch settlers. Michigan celery is produced on black organic soil called "muck". According to the Michigan Celery Promotion Co-Operative, Michigan ranks third in production of celery in this country.

For the most intense celery flavor, choose stalks with the most green color. The stalks with less color will be mild flavored and may be preferred for eating raw.

HOW MUCH TO BUY??? 1 pound of celery is usually about 2 bunches and will yield 2 -2 1/2 cups of cooked celery.

SELECTION: Choose unblemished celery which looks fresh and crisp, with light green or medium green stalks. The stalks should have a glossy surface and be crisp enough to snap easily.

AVOID: Celery with cuts, bruises or other damage should be avoided. Also avoid wilted, pithy or discolored celery.

STORAGE: At home, trim and rinse celery. After shaking off extra water, place celery in a plastic bag and store in the refrigerator. Limp celery can be freshened up by being placed in ice-cold water for several minutes. Celery should keep well in the refrigerator for 1 to 2 weeks.

This delicious dressing contains absolutely no oil. Serve it on tossed salad for extra flavor without many extra calories.

CELERY SALAD DRESSING
Yield: about 1 1/2 cups

2 cups celery cut in 1/2-inch pieces
1/4 cup scallions (green onions) cut in 1-inch pieces
2 tablespoons sugar
1/2 teaspoon salt
1/8 teaspoon ground black pepper
3 tablespoons cider vinegar
3 tablespoons water

◊ In the bowl of a food processor fitted with a metal wing blade or in an electric blender, process celery, scallions, sugar, salt, black pepper, vinegar and water until smooth.
◊ Serve over sliced tomatoes, spinach or other salad greens, if desired.
◊ May be made 24 hours before serving, covered and refrigerated. Stir before using.

American Celery Council
New York, New York

PORK CHOW MEIN
Yield: 6 servings

1 lb. boneless pork
3 tablespoons vegetable oil
1 cup sliced green onion
1 cup sliced celery
2 cups sliced fresh mushrooms
1 (8 oz.) can water chestnuts, drained and sliced
1 (13 3/4 oz.) can chicken broth
1/4 cup soy sauce
1 (16 oz.) can chop suey vegetables, drained
3 tablespoons cornstarch
Hot, cooked rice

◊ Partially freeze pork; slice thinly across the grain into bite-size strips.
◊ Preheat a large skillet or wok; add vegetable oil. Add the pork; stir-fry 2 to 3 minutes. Remove meat.
◊ Add onion and celery to skillet or wok. Stir-fry 1 minute. Add mushrooms and water chestnuts; stir-fry 1 minute.
◊ Add 1 1/4 cups of the chicken broth, the soy sauce and chop suey vegetables. Add meat to vegetable mixture.
◊ Stir remaining chicken broth into cornstarch. Stir into meat-vegetable mixture. Cook and stir till thickened and bubbly. Cook and stir 1 to 2 minutes more. Serve over hot cooked rice.

Thorn Apple Valley, Inc.
Southfield, Michigan

47

CELERY STUFFING
Yield: 3-4 cups stuffing

1 1/2 cups chopped celery
1/2 cup chopped onion
2 tablespoons butter or margarine
1/2 teaspoon salt
1/4 teaspoon ground pepper
1/2 teaspoon poultry seasoning
1/2 teaspoon ground sage
4 cups dry bread cubes or stuffing croutons
1/2 cup chicken broth or water

◊ Preheat oven to 325° F.
◊ Using medium heat, sauté celery and onion in butter or margarine until tender. Stir in salt, pepper, poultry seasoning and sage. Toss with bread cubes until combined. Pour broth or water over mixture and stir until blended. Spoon into greased 1 1/2 quart casserole.
◊ Bake at 325° for 35 to 45 minutes, or until hot.
◊ NOTE: Instead of baking the stuffing as a side dish, it may be used for stuffing poultry. This makes enough stuffing to stuff a 4 to 5-pound chicken. The recipe may be doubled for one 10-12 pound turkey. Be sure to remove any leftover stuffing from poultry and refrigerate stuffing immediately after the meal.

Give this tasty sandwich a try. Use your favorite cheese for this sandwich. We especially like Muenster and Cheddar.

TURKEY SALAD SUBMARINES
Yield: 4 large sandwiches

3/4 cup mayonnaise or salad dressing
1/4 teaspoon ground black pepper
1/4 cup toasted, slivered almonds
1 cup chopped celery
2 cups turkey, cooked and chopped into small cubes
4 submarine sandwich buns
Sliced tomatoes
Sliced cheese
Alfalfa sprouts

◊ Stir mayonnaise and pepper together in a medium bowl. Fold in almonds, celery and turkey. Spread one-fourth of the turkey salad on each bun.
◊ Top sandwiches with tomatoes, cheese and sprouts, as desired.
◊ NOTE: To toast almonds, spread a thin layer of almonds on a cookie sheet. Place in 350° oven for a few minutes until lightly toasted. Watch the almonds closely to avoid burned almonds!

CELERY

This yummy recipe is modeled after a cheese ball recipe. However, your guests will find it much easier to pick up the stuffed celery and go than it is to spread cheese on a cracker. Plus, celery has hardly any calories!

CHEESE STUFFED CELERY
Yield: 1 1/2 to 2 cups cheese spread

1 (8 oz.) pkg. cream cheese
1 teaspoon Worcestershire sauce
2 tablespoons milk
2 cups (8 oz.) shredded Cheddar cheese
1/2 cup chopped radishes
1/2 cup chopped green pepper
Celery stalks

◊ Beat together cream cheese, Worcestershire sauce and milk. Stir in Cheddar cheese, chopped radishes and chopped green pepper.
◊ Clean celery stalks and remove leafy ends. Spread cheese mixture in each stalk. Cut each stalk into 2 to 3-inch long pieces. Serve.

CHERRIES

MAJOR GROWING AREAS

Michigan is one the top cherry producing states in the country. In fact, Traverse City is known as the "Cherry Capital of the World". Michigan is this nation's top producer of tart cherries. The many sweet cherries harvested in the state place Michigan around 4th for sweet cherry production. Most of the cherries produced in the state are processed commercially.

Weather conditions in the spring are crucial for the growth of the blossoms into ripe cherries. Most of the cherry trees are located near the Lake Michigan shoreline where the spring weather is tempered by the lake. The harvest season for cherries is short. Harvest begins in early July and is nearly finished by mid-August.

Tart cherries are typically used in pies and commercially prepared pie fillings. Look for frozen, canned or dried tart cherries or for cherry juice. Sweet cherries can be found frozen or canned year round and can be used in sauces, cakes, over ice cream, or many other ways.

HOW MUCH TO BUY??? One pound of cherries will yield 2 to 2 1/2 cups pitted cherries. Plan on 1 pound of cherries to serve 4 people.

SELECTION: Cherries should be plump with bright, glossy surfaces and the stem should be fresh looking. Color of cherries will depend on the variety.

AVOID: Cherries which have a sticky surface may be overripe and should be avoided. Discard fruit which is shriveled or shows signs of decay such as mold or brown discoloration.

STORAGE: Do not wash cherries until just before using them. Store cherries uncovered in the refrigerator and use them as quickly as possible. Cherries will store longer with the stem intact. For best flavor, use cherries within 3 or 4 days. Cherries may be canned or frozen for longer storage.

Each year cherry grower families in Grand Traverse, Leelanau, Benzie and Antrim counties prepare an array of cherry desserts for the "Very Cherry Luncheon". The luncheon is coordinated through the Michigan State University Cooperative Extension Service and The National Cherry Festival. This wonderful cake recipe is from the "Very Cherry Luncheon" recipe book sent to us by the Michigan State University Cooperative Extension Service. This cake is not real sweet, but has a rich flavor. It was even a hit with those in our tasting group who aren't wild about cherries. Try it the next time you need a special dessert.

ALMOND CAKE WITH CHERRIES
Yield: 12 servings

1 cup blanched almonds
1 1/3 cups sugar, divided
1 cup all-purpose flour
8 tablespoons butter or margarine
2 tablespoons Amaretto liqueur
8 egg whites
Pinch salt
**1 (10 oz.) package frozen sweet cherries (pitted), thawed and
   drained**
1/2 tablespoon powdered sugar

◊ Preheat oven to 350° F.
◊ Butter a 9-inch springform pan. Line bottom with waxed paper and butter the paper. Grind almonds and 1 cup sugar to a powder. Combine with the flour.
◊ Melt butter and add Amaretto.
◊ Beat egg whites with salt until they hold soft peaks. Gradually beat remaining 1/3 cup sugar into egg whites until they hold soft peaks.
◊ Fold almond mixture into egg whites 1/4 at a time, alternating with additions of the butter mixture. Pour into prepared pan. Gently press cherries into top of cake without pushing all the way in.

ALMOND CAKE WITH CHERRIES (cont.)

◊ Bake 45 - 50 minutes, or until a toothpick inserted in center comes out clean. Cool, unmold and dust with powdered sugar.

Very Cherry Luncheon
Sponsored by Michigan State University Cooperative Extension Service and The National Cherry Festival

CHERRIES 'N' CREAM
Yield: 1 cup dip

Michigan Fresh Sweet Cherries, with or without stems
1 cup dairy sour cream
2 tablespoons powdered sugar
1 tablespoon lemon juice
1/2 teaspoon grated orange peel

◊ Rinse fresh cherries and drain well.
◊ In a small bowl, combine sour cream, sugar, lemon juice and orange peel; mix well.
◊ Transfer sour cream mixture to a small serving bowl. Serve with fresh cherries as a summer snack or dessert.

Cherry Marketing Institute, Inc.
Okemos, Michigan

This recipe was a winner in the Michigan "Super Bowl" recipe contest. Our thanks to Dave and Gale Phillips for sharing it with us. Dave notes that this soup can be eaten year round. Served hot, it's great for cold winter mornings; hearty and nourishing with homemade cinnamon toast. Served cold, it is refreshing and nourishing for hot summer mornings. No matter what time of the year, the whole house smells wonderful while the soup is cooking!

MICHIGAN MORNING FRUIT SOUP
Yield: 8 - 6 oz. portions

1 cup diced carrot
1/2 cup diced celery
1/2 cup diced onion
8 cups water
3/4 cup MICHIGAN apple juice
3/4 cup MICHIGAN cherry juice
2 tablespoons brown sugar
2 tablespoons lemon juice
1 1/4 teaspoon salt
Pinch of ground cinnamon and ginger
Small pinch of ground nutmeg
1/2 cup diced MICHIGAN red delicious apple
1/2 cup diced MICHIGAN golden delicious apple
1/2 cup diced MICHIGAN peaches
1/2 cup diced MICHIGAN pears
1/2 cup diced MICHIGAN dark sweet cherries
1/4 cup diced MICHIGAN blueberries
1 1/2 tablespoons cornstarch
1 piece thickly sliced bread
Melted butter or margarine
Cinnamon and sugar

◊ Place carrot, celery, onion and water in stainless steel pot, and bring to a boil. Then simmer for 20 minutes. Remove from heat and strain. Discard the vegetables, saving only the stock.

MICHIGAN MORNING SOUP (cont.)

Add apple juice, cherry juice, brown sugar, lemon juice, salt and spices. Return to the stove and bring to a simmer for 10 minutes. Add fruits. Bring to a boil, and simmer for another 10 minutes. Strain, separating the cooked fruits from the stock. Place cooked fruits in a food processor and bring to a coarse, lumpy blend. Next, mix the cornstarch with a small amount of water and use it to thicken the stock. Lastly, add fruit mixture to thicken the stock.

◊ Toast the bread. Brush with butter, and sprinkle with cinnamon and sugar. Cut into rings. Float on soup for garnish.

◊ HINTS: * Do not peel fruits, as the skin adds to the flavor.
　　　　　 * Wonderful for brunch or as an elegant appetizer for a gourmet dinner.

Dave and Gale Phillips
Wharfside
Charlevoix, Michigan

DRIED CHERRY SAUCE
Yield: 1 cup sauce

1/2 cup butter
1/3 cup dried cherries
1/4 cup whipping cream
1/2 cup dry white wine
1/8 teaspoon ground cardamom

◊ Process butter and cherries in food processor until smooth consistency; chill until firm.

◊ Combine cream and wine in saucepan. Bring to a boil and reduce to 1/3 cup. Add cardamom. Whisk in cherry-butter by tablespoons. Serve sauce with veal medallions.

◊ NOTE: Dried cherries can be found in gourmet or specialty shops.

Graceland Fruit Co-op
Frankfort, Michigan

CHERRIES

CHERRY KUCHEN
Yield: 15 servings

Topping:
3/4 cup light brown sugar, firmly packed
1/2 cup all-purpose flour
1/2 cup instant oats
1 teaspoon ground cinnamon
1/4 teaspoon ground nutmeg
1/3 cup butter or margarine, softened

Batter:
1 1/2 cups all-purpose flour
1/2 cup sugar
2 teaspoons baking powder
1/2 teaspoon salt
3 tablespoons butter or margarine
2 eggs
3/4 cup milk
1 (21 ounce) can cherry filling and topping

◊ Preheat oven to 350° F.
◊ For the topping: In a medium mixing bowl, combine sugar, flour, oats, cinnamon and nutmeg; mix well. Cut in butter to make a crumbly mixture; set aside.
◊ For the batter: In a large mixing bowl, combine flour, sugar, baking powder and salt. Cut in butter until mixture resembles coarse crumbs. Add eggs and milk; mix just until the dry ingredients are moistened. Do not overmix; batter will be lumpy.
◊ Spread half the batter into a lightly greased 13 x 9 x 2-inch baking pan. Spoon cherry filling evenly over batter. Top with remaining batter. Sprinkle reserved topping over batter. Bake in 350° oven for 30 to 35 minutes, or until top springs back when lightly pressed with finger.

Cherry Marketing Institute, Inc.
Okemos, Michigan

56

CHERRY CREAM DESSERT
Yield: 12 to15 servings

1 1/2 cups graham cracker crumbs
2 tablespoons sugar
1/2 cup butter or margarine, melted
1 pint (2 cups) very cold whipping cream
1/2 cup powdered sugar
1 (8 oz.) package cream cheese, softened
1 (21 oz.) can cherry pie filling and topping

◊ Mix graham cracker crumbs, sugar and melted butter. Press into bottom of lightly greased 9x13-inch pan.
◊ Beat whipping cream together with powdered sugar until cream is fluffy and soft peaks form. Add softened cream cheese. Continue to beat until smooth and well-blended.
◊ Spread over crumb crust. Spoon cherry pie filling over cream cheese layer. Chill until serving.

CHERRY WINKS
Yield: about 5 dozen cookies

2 1/4 cups all-purpose flour
2 teaspoons baking powder
1/2 teaspoon salt
3/4 cup margarine or butter, softened
1 cup sugar
2 eggs
2 tablespoons milk
1 teaspoon vanilla flavoring
1 cup chopped nuts
1 cup finely cut, pitted dates
1/3 cup finely chopped maraschino cherries
2 2/3 cups Kellogg's Corn Flakes® cereal, crushed to measure 1 1/3 cups
15 maraschino cherries, cut into quarters

◊ Stir together flour, baking powder and salt; set aside.
◊ In large mixing bowl, beat margarine and sugar until light and fluffy. Add eggs. Beat well. Stir in milk and vanilla. Add flour mixture. Mix until well combined. Stir in nuts, dates and chopped cherries.
◊ Portion dough using level measuring-tablespoon. Shape into balls. Roll in crushed Kellogg's Corn Flakes cereal. Place about 2 inches apart on greased baking sheets. Top each with cherry quarter.
◊ Bake at 350° F about 10 minutes or until lightly browned. Remove immediately from baking sheets. Cool on wire rack.

Kellogg Company
Battle Creek, Michigan

58

TART CHERRY ALMOND BREAD
Yield: 1 loaf

3 cups all-purpose flour
2 teaspoons baking powder
1 teaspoon baking soda
1/2 teaspoon salt
1/4 cup butter or margarine, softened
1 cup sugar
2 eggs
1 cup buttermilk
2 teaspoons almond extract
1 cup pitted tart cherries, drained
1 teaspoon sugar
3 tablespoons sliced almonds

◊ Preheat oven to 350° F. Combine flour, baking powder, baking soda and salt. Set aside.

◊ In a large bowl, beat together butter and 1 cup sugar. Add eggs and mix well. Stir in buttermilk and almond extract. Stir in flour mixture. Chop drained cherries; stir into batter.

◊ Spread batter in greased 9 x 5-inch loaf pan. Sprinkle 1 teaspoon sugar and sliced almonds over batter. Bake at 350° for 70 minutes, or until toothpick inserted in center comes out clean. Cool 10 minutes, then turn out of pan onto cooling rack.

59

CHERRIED PORK CHOPS
Yield: 4 to 6 servings

4 - 6 pork chops
1/2 cup sherry
4 teaspoons paprika
2/3 cup all-purpose flour
2 tablespoons shortening
1 tablespoon cornstarch
1/2 cup brown sugar, firmly packed
1/2 cup lemon juice
1 (16 oz.) can dark sweet cherries, with liquid
1 clove garlic, crushed
1 teaspoon ground ginger
1 teaspoon crushed basil leaves
1 teaspoon ground oregano
2 teaspoons salt
Hot, cooked rice
2 oranges, peeled and sliced (for garnish)

◊ Trim chops of excess fat. Marinate chops in sherry for one
  hour; drain, reserving sherry.
◊ Season chops with paprika; dip in flour; brown in shortening,
  using large skillet. Drain excess fat. Combine cornstarch,
  brown sugar, sherry and lemon juice to make a smooth paste.
  Add undrained cherries, garlic, ginger, basil, oregano, and salt;
  blend well. Pour over chops. Cover skillet and cook slowly 30
  to 45 minutes, until meat is tender. Serve over rice. Garnish
  with orange slices.

Burnette Foods Inc.
Producers of Mother's Maid®
Elk Rapids, Michigan

AMERICAN SPOON CHERRY PECAN MUFFINS
Yield: 12 muffins

2 cups all-purpose flour
1/2 teaspoon salt
1/4 cup granulated sugar
2 teaspoons baking powder
2 large eggs, lightly beaten
1/2 cup (1 stick) sweet butter, melted and cooled
3/4 cup milk
1 teaspoon vanilla extract
1 cup (4 oz.) pecans, coarsely chopped
1 cup (4 oz.) dried red tart cherries
Finely grated rind of one lemon

◊ Preheat the oven to 400° F.
◊ Lightly grease the muffin pans.
◊ In a large bowl, stir together the flour, salt, sugar and baking powder.
◊ In another bowl, combine the eggs, butter, milk and vanilla and mix well.
◊ Pour the egg mixture into the dry mixture, add the pecans, cherries, and lemon rind, and stir until just blended.
◊ Spoon the batter into the greased muffin pans and bake for 20 minutes, or until golden and a cake tester inserted into the center of a muffin comes out clean.
◊ NOTE: Dried cherries can be found in gourmet or specialty shops.

Christine Unger Schefman for
American Spoon Foods
Petoskey, Michigan

HEAVENLY CHERRY ANGEL FOOD TRIFLE
Yield: 8 to 10 servings

5 cups angel food cake cubes
1/4 cup cherry liqueur, optional
1 cup powdered sugar
1 (3 oz.) pkg. cream cheese, softened
1 (8 oz.) pkg. frozen non-dairy whipped topping, thawed and divided
1/2 cup toasted chopped pecans
1 (21 oz.) can cherry filling or topping

◊ Place cake cubes in large bowl. Sprinkle with liqueur, if desired; let stand 30 minutes.
◊ In medium bowl, combine powdered sugar and cream cheese; beat until blended.
◊ Reserve 2 tablespoons whipped topping; fold remaining topping into cheese mixture. Stir topping mixture and pecans into cake cubes; mix well.
◊ Spoon cake mixture into a pretty glass or crystal bowl. Spread cherry filling evenly on top. (Or if desired layer one-half cake mixture and cherry filling. Repeat layers.)
◊ Cover and refrigerate at least 3 hours. Garnish servings with reserved whipped topping.

Martha Schaub
Manitou Market and Bakery
Lake Leelanau, Michigan

BROILED CHICKEN "LITTLE TRAVERSE BAY"
Yield: 6 servings

1 (6.25 oz.) package Uncle Ben's long grain and wild rice
  mix
1/3 cup toasted walnut pieces
1/3 cup dried cherries
6 (8 oz. each) boneless chicken breasts with skin
Salt
Melted butter or margarine
Warm brandied peach sauce (or your favorite sauce)

◊ Prepare rice mix according to package directions. Stir in
  walnuts and dried cherries.
◊ Place a chicken breast skin side down in between 2 pieces of
  plastic wrap. Using flat side of a large meat cleaver, gently
  pound breast meat. Repeat with remaining breasts.
◊ Sprinkle meat with salt, as desired. Place 1/2 cup rice mixture
  in center of each chicken breast and fold under side corners to
  center and form a ball.
◊ Place breasts on buttered broiler pan. Broil until thoroughly
  cooked and golden brown, about 10 to 15 minutes.
◊ Baste each breast with warm peach sauce just before serving.
◊ NOTE: Dried cherries can be found in gourmet or specialty
  shops.

Schuler's, Inc.
Marshall, Michigan

63

MICHIGAN CHERRY PIE
Yield: 1, 9-inch pie

2 (16 oz. each) cans pitted tart cherries, with liquid
1 cup sugar
1/3 cup all-purpose flour
1/4 teaspoon cinnamon
1/4 teaspoon red food coloring
Unbaked pastry for a 2-crust, 9-inch pie
2 tablespoons butter or margarine

◊ Preheat oven to 400° F.
◊ Drain liquid from cherries, reserving 1/2 cup juice. Combine
  1/2 cup juice, sugar, flour, cinnamon and food coloring. Stir in
  cherries.
◊ Line 9-inch pie plate with pastry. Fill pastry with cherry mixture.
◊ Dot with butter or margarine.
◊ Place top crust on pie and seal. Cut slits in crust for steam to
  escape. Bake in 400° oven for 50 to 55 minutes, or until filling
  is bubbling and crust is golden brown.

CORN (SWEET & POPCORN)

MAJOR GROWING AREAS

The wonderful taste of fresh corn on the cob makes it worth a special trip to the market for the freshest corn possible. Always cook sweet corn as soon as possible after picking. The sugar in sweet corn starts turning to starch after picking, so it is sweetest right after picking. In Michigan, fresh sweet corn is usually harvested during the months of July, August, and September.

If possible, puncture a kernel of corn near the top of the ear to check for ripeness. On a ripe ear, the juice will be a milky liquid. On an immature ear, the juice will be clear. If the ear is past it's prime, the kernel will be tough and dry.

For a special treat, look for the new extra sweet varieties of sweet corn. These hybrids have a higher sugar content than other varieties, which means they have a sweeter flavor.

To prepare corn before cooking, remove the husks and silk. If necessary, cut off the stem. Salt may toughen corn during cooking, so salt corn after cooking. Fresh corn may be cooked in boiling water, microwaved, or grilled in the husk.

Ears of popcorn are smaller than sweet or field corn. The entire process of growing, harvesting, drying and storing popcorn is more difficult than it is for other corn. Most of us would agree that the extra effort is worth it. Popcorn continues to be one of the top snack foods in this country.

SELECTION: Choose sweet corn with a fresh, grass green colored, tightly wrapped husk. The ear should be free from decay or worm injury. The stem end of the corn should be moist, not dried out. Select ears evenly covered with plump, tender kernels.

65

CORN (SWEET & POPCORN)

AVOID: Check the outer husk on the ear of corn. Avoid those husks that are dry and wilted or are yellowish in color. The stem end of the ear should not be dried out. Do not choose ears of corn with underdeveloped or overdeveloped kernels. Depressed areas on the kernels indicate the corn is past it's prime.

STORAGE: Popcorn will store well for 2 years in an airtight container.

Sweet corn should be cooked and served as quickly as possible after it is picked. If the sweet corn must be stored, place the unhusked ears in the coolest part of the refrigerator. Use corn within a day or two if possible.

For best flavor, sweet corn should be blanched before freezing. When canning corn, a pressure cooker must always be used.

Spice up corn on the cob with this butter, or use a few tablespoons to add extra flavor to canned or frozen cut corn.

CHILI BUTTER FOR CORN ON THE COB
Yield: 1/2 cup butter

1/2 cup (1 stick) butter or margarine
3 green onions, finely chopped
1 clove garlic, minced
1 tablespoon chili powder
1/2 teaspoon lemon juice
1 teaspoon salt
10 to 12 ears fresh sweet corn, cooked and drained

◊ Combine butter, green onions, garlic, chili powder, lemon juice and salt. Beat with mixer or process in food processor until mixture is smooth.
◊ Rub a few teaspoons of chili butter over kernels on each ear of corn just before serving.
◊ Cover and refrigerate any leftover chili butter.

When the first ears of corn are finally harvested, fresh off the cob is the only way to eat it! However, by the end of the season, when you are ready for something different, Fresh Creamed Corn is a delicious way to serve corn.

FRESH CREAMED CORN
Yield: 2 servings

**2 ears corn
2 tablespoons butter or margarine
1/3 cup finely chopped onion
1 tablespoon all-purpose flour
1 (5 oz.) can evaporated milk
Salt
Pepper**

◊ Add corn to large pot of boiling water. Cook for 5 minutes. Drain corn and rinse with cold water until corn is cool. Cut kernels from cob. Set aside.
◊ Melt butter in a saucepan. Add onion and sauté over low heat until onion is tender. Stir in flour. Slowly add the evaporated milk. Continue stirring and cooking until the mixture thickens.
◊ Add corn to thickened milk mixture and season to taste with salt and pepper. Continue cooking until corn is heated. Serve immediately.

MICROWAVE DIRECTIONS:
◊ Add corn to large pot of boiling water on stove. Cook for 5 minutes. Drain corn and rinse with cold water until corn is cool. Cut kernels from cob. Set aside.
◊ Place butter in 1-quart casserole. Microwave in high power for 30 to 45 seconds, or until melted. Add onion. Cook, covered, on high power for 2 to 3 minutes, or until onion is tender. Stir in flour. Slowly add the evaporated milk. Cook on high power for 2 to 3 minutes, or until thickened. Stir twice during cooking time.
◊ Add corn to thickened milk mixture and season to taste with salt and pepper. Cook on high power for 1 minute, or until corn is heated. Stir halfway through cooking time. Serve immediately.

COUNTRY CORN CHOWDER
Yield: 8 servings

1/4 cup butter or margarine
1 medium onion, chopped
1/4 cup all-purpose flour
1 1/2 cups milk
2 (12 oz. each) cans evaporated milk
1 teaspoon salt
1 teaspoon instant chicken bouillon (or 1 cube, crushed)
1/8 teaspoon pepper
2 (16 oz. each) cans cream-style corn
4 slices bacon, cooked and crumbled

◊ In large saucepan, melt butter and sauté onion in butter until
tender. Stir in the flour.
◊ Add milk and evaporated milk. Continue cooking over medium
heat until smooth and thickened, stirring continuously.
◊ Add salt, chicken bouillon, pepper, cream-style corn and
bacon. Heat until very warm, but do not boil. Serve warm.

MICROWAVE DIRECTIONS:
◊ Place butter and onion in 3-quart casserole dish. Cook,
covered, on high power for 3 to 4 minutes, or until onions are
tender. Stir in the flour. Add milk and evaporated milk. Cook
on high power for 10 to 12 minutes, or until smooth and thickened. Stir 3-4 times during cooking time.
◊ Add salt, chicken bouillon, pepper, cream-style corn and
bacon. Cook on high power for 4 to 5 minutes, or until hot. Stir
1 to 2 times during cooking time. Do not allow mixture to boil.

This recipe is from my grandmother's recipe file. It's a good recipe for those of us who like to keep things simple, and it does taste good.

SCALLOPED CORN
Yield: 4 servings

2 cups corn, cooked and drained
1 cup milk
2 tablespoons sugar
1 tablespoon all-purpose flour
2 tablespoons butter or margarine, melted
2 eggs
1 teaspoon salt

◊ Preheat oven to 350° F.
◊ Place corn in buttered 1-quart casserole dish.
◊ In a small bowl, combine milk, sugar, flour, butter, eggs and salt. Stir until blended. Pour over corn.
◊ Bake at 350° for 60 minutes, or until mixture is set and top is golden brown.

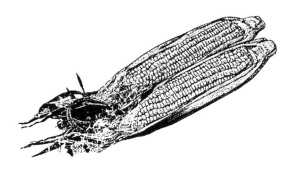

IRRESISTIBLE M & M CORN CRUNCH
Yield: 3 quarts

2 quarts popped popcorn
2 cups peanuts
1 (8 oz.) package M & M chocolate candies
1/2 cup light corn syrup
1 1/2 cups sugar
1 cup butter or margarine

◊ Combine popcorn, peanuts and M & M's in a large bowl. Set aside.
◊ Combine syrup, sugar and butter in medium saucepan. Bring mixture to a boil, stirring often.
◊ Continue boiling mixture and stirring often until hard ball stage (250-265° F) is reached. Pour syrup over popcorn mixture and stir until evenly coated.
◊ Spread on greased jelly roll pan. When cool, break into pieces.

SOUTH OF THE BORDER POPCORN SPRINKLE
Yield: 1/3 cup seasoned salt

1/4 cup salt or popcorn salt
2 teaspoons chili powder
2 teaspoons butter flavored sprinkles
1/2 teaspoon cumin
1 teaspoon paprika
Hot, freshly popped corn

◊ In a small bowl, combine salt, chili powder, butter flavored sprinkles, cumin and paprika. Stir until mixed. Transfer to container with shaker top.
◊ Sprinkle over hot, freshly popped corn as desired. Store extra in an air tight container at room temperature.

CUCUMBERS

MAJOR GROWING AREAS

Michigan is this country's #1 state in pickling cucumber production. Many cucumbers are also raised to be sold as fresh market cucumbers. Typically, fresh slicing cucumbers are available from July through September. Fresh pickling cucumbers are available for a shorter time. Naturally, home or commercially processed pickles can be enjoyed throughout the year.

Fresh, tender cucumbers may be used without peeling. On older cucumbers, the peel may become bitter flavored. Slicing cucumbers in the store are sometimes coated with an edible wax to preserve freshness. Cut off a thin slice of the cucumber and taste it. If the peel tastes bitter, you may want to peel the cucumber before using it.

HOW MUCH TO BUY??? 1 medium cucumber serves two people and weighs 1/2 pound or slightly less.

SELECTION: Choose cucumbers that are firm, well shaped, and a good green color. Pickling cucumbers are generally 2 to 6 inches in length and slicing cucumbers should be about 6 to 10 inches with an average to small diameter.

AVOID: Overgrown, large diameter cucumbers should be avoided. Discard cucumbers with shriveled or withered ends as they may be bitter. Older cucumbers become dull green or yellow and won't taste as fresh.

STORAGE: Keep cucumbers wrapped in plastic, or in the crisper drawer, in the refrigerator. The quality of cucumbers deteriorates quickly, so cucumbers should be used in 3 to 5 days.

71

SOUR CREAM CUCUMBERS
Yield: 8 servings

2 medium cucumbers, thinly sliced
1 small onion, thinly sliced
1/2 cup dairy sour cream
1 tablespoon vinegar
1 teaspoon sugar
1/2 teaspoon salt

◊ Combine the cucumbers and onion. Stir together sour cream,
  vinegar, sugar and salt; toss with vegetables. Cover and chill,
  stirring occasionally.

Meijer , Inc.
Grand Rapids, Michigan

The nice thing about this lettuce salad is that it can be made ahead and left in the refrigerator until serving time. Give it a quick toss and you have a crisp lettuce salad when it is time to eat!

MAKE AHEAD MICHIGAN SALAD
Yield: 6 servings

1 head iceberg lettuce (about 4 cups)
1 cucumber
1 carrot, chopped
1 stalk celery, chopped
1/4 cup mayonnaise or salad dressing
1 tablespoon sugar
4 strips bacon, cooked and crumbled

◊ Tear or slice lettuce into bite-size pieces. Divide torn lettuce into thirds. Peel cucumber and cut in half lengthwise. Cut each cucumber half in to thin slices.

◊ In a deep bowl, layer vegetables in the following order: 1/3 of lettuce, sliced cucumbers, 1/3 lettuce, chopped carrots and celery, 1/3 lettuce.

◊ Spread mayonnaise or salad dressing in a thin layer over lettuce. Sprinkle sugar over mayonnaise. Sprinkle crumbled bacon over top of salad. Cover tightly and refrigerate for a few hours before serving. (May also be made the night before serving.)

◊ Toss salad just before serving.

MISS LIZZIE'S TASTY TUNA SALAD
Yield: 4 servings

1 (6 1/2 oz.) can tuna packed in spring water, drained
2 medium boiled eggs, chopped
1/4 cup Aunt Jane's Sweet Pickles or Sweet Pickle Cubes,
   chopped
1 tablespoon finely chopped onion
4 tablespoons mayonnaise or salad dressing
Salt and pepper to taste

◊ Mix together tuna, eggs, sweet pickles, onion, mayonnaise and
  seasonings. Chill at least 30 minutes before serving.
◊ Scoop onto lettuce leaves with ice cream scoop and flank with
  Aunt Jane's Kosher Icebergs.

Aunt Jane's Food, Inc.
Croswell, Michigan

CUCUMBER DIP
Yield: About 1 1/2 cups dip

1 (8 oz.) carton cream cheese with chives and onion
1/3 cup mayonnaise or salad dressing
1/4 teaspoon hot pepper sauce
1 medium cucumber, peeled, seeded and finely chopped

◊ Stir together cream cheese, mayonnaise or salad dressing,
  and pepper sauce.
◊ Stir in chopped cucumbers. Cover and chill.
◊ Serve with cut-up fresh vegetables or crackers.

PERFECT PARTY TRIANGLES
Yield: 12 to 15 servings

1 (8 oz.) package cream cheese
1 (0.4 oz) package Hidden Valley Salad Dressing Mix
1 loaf party cocktail bread
1 - 2 cucumbers

◊ Beat cream cheese and salad dressing mix until mixture is smooth and creamy.
◊ Spread cream cheese mixture on slices of bread. (Each slice will make 2 triangles, so prepare as many as needed.)
◊ Peel and thinly slice a cucumber (or 2 if needed). Top each slice of bread with a cucumber slice. Cut each slice of bread diagonally to make 2 triangles. Serve.

MISS IDA'S DILLED POTATO SALAD
Yield: 12 servings

1/3 cup Aunt Jane's Dill Pickle juice
2 tablespoons olive oil (optional)
7 medium potatoes cooked in skins, peeled and sliced
1/2 cup chopped Aunt Jane's Dill Pickles
1/3 cup sliced green onions
4 medium boiled eggs, peeled
1 cup mayonnaise or salad dressing
1/2 cup dairy sour cream (plain yogurt may be substituted)
2 teaspoons Dijon mustard
Garlic salt
Celery seed
Black pepper

◊ Pour pickle juice mixed with olive oil over warm potatoes and
   chill for 2 hours.
◊ Add chopped pickles, onion and chopped egg whites. Sieve
   yolks, mix with mayonnaise, sour cream and mustard and fold
   into salad. Add garlic salt, celery seed and pepper to taste.
   Chill 2 hours.
◊ Scoop into lettuce leaves with ice cream scoop.

Aunt Jane's Food, Inc.
Croswell, Michigan

DRY BEANS

Dry beans from Michigan are available world-wide. Michigan typically is the nation's top producer of dry beans. Many different varieties of dry beans are raised in Michigan. According to the Michigan Bean Commission, Michigan is the top producer of navy, cranberry and black turtle beans in the U.S. Other varieties of Michigan beans include pinto and kidney beans.

MAJOR GROWING AREAS

Low in fat, navy beans have no cholesterol. Dry beans are a very good source of fiber and a good (though not complete) source of protein. Since the protein is incomplete, dry beans should be combined with other foods to provide all of the essential amino acids our bodies need. For example, dry beans can be combined with small amounts of meat, poultry, fish, or eggs to provide all amino acids. Dry beans may also be combined with seeds, grains, or small amounts of dairy products.

A can or jar of pre-cooked beans is ready to be used in recipes as soon as the container is opened. Dry beans must be soaked and then cooked. There are different methods for soaking beans. They may be soaked overnight in a water and salt mixture. For a quicker method, beans may be cooked a short time in boiling water and then allowed to soak for an hour. Follow the soaking directions on the package of the dry beans. Beans should then simmered in water for 2 hours, or until they are tender.

HOW MUCH TO BUY??? There are about 2 cups of dry beans in a pound of beans. One pound of dry navy beans will yield 5 1/2 to 6 cups cooked beans. A one pound can of cooked beans will be a little less than 2 cups of beans.

STORAGE: Dry beans should be stored in their original package or a covered container in a dry, cool location. They will keep almost indefinitely. Canned beans may be stored up to a year and should also be stored in a cool, dry area. Store cooked beans in a covered container in the refrigerator and use within a few days. Cooked beans may also be frozen and will store well for 6 months.

SATURDAY NIGHT SUPPER
Yield: 4 servings

4 center cut pork chops, thin-sliced
1 (1 lb. 14 oz.) can baked beans, or 3 cups baked beans
2 tablespoons apple jelly
2 teaspoons water
8 slices, pared apple
Cinnamon

◊ In a skillet, brown chops about 10 minutes per side; drain. Pour beans into 2 quart casserole and place chops on top of beans. Cover and bake at 350° F for 45 minutes.
◊ In a small bowl, combine jelly and water. Baste chops with this mixture and arrange apple slices on top. Sprinkle with cinnamon. Return to oven and bake another 15 minutes, uncovered. Serve warm.

The Michigan Bean Commission
Leslie, Michigan

CHILI BEAN SOUP
Yield: 6 to 8 servings

1 1/2 pounds ground round
1 large onion, chopped
1 1/2 cups water
2 (8 oz.) cans tomato sauce
1 (1 lb., 12 oz.) can tomatoes, with liquid
1 green bell pepper, chopped
1/2 teaspoon garlic powder
2 tablespoons chili powder
Salt
Pepper
1 (24 oz.) jar Randall Pinto Beans, with liquid

◊ In a large pot, brown ground round until crumbly. Drain off fat. Add onion, water, tomato sauce, tomatoes, green pepper, garlic powder and chili powder. Season to taste with salt and black pepper.

◊ Simmer mixture for 1 hour, or until flavors are blended and vegetables are tender. Add beans and cook until beans are hot.

Randall Food Products, Inc.
Tekonsha, Michigan

79

This thick, hearty casserole hits the spot after a day of sledding or skiing on the Michigan slopes.

HAM AND BEAN BAKE
Yield: 6 to 8 servings

1 medium onion, chopped
2 tablespoons butter or margarine
1 clove garlic, minced
1/4 teaspoon ground pepper
Dash ground cloves
2 cups cubed fully cooked ham
1 (48 oz.) jar Great Northern beans, with liquid
1/4 cup water

◊ Sauté onions in butter in small skillet. Stir in garlic, pepper and cloves.
◊ Stir together onion mixture, ham, beans, and water. Turn into a 2 or 3-quart casserole. Bake, covered, at 350° F for 45 minutes.
◊ Uncover and bake 40 to 45 minutes longer, stirring occasionally, until mixture is heated through.
◊ Serve bowls of hot casserole with cornbread.

CITY SLICKER BEANS
Yield: 6 servings

1 (1 lb.) can lima beans, drained
1 (1 lb.) can kidney beans, drained
1 (1 lb.) can navy beans, drained
3 small onions, chopped
1 clove garlic, minced
3 tablespoons vegetable oil or bacon drippings
1/2 cup catsup
3 tablespoons brown sugar
3 tablespoons cider vinegar
1 teaspoon salt
1 teaspoon dry mustard
1/4 teaspoon ground black pepper

◊ Combine lima beans, kidney beans, navy beans, onion and garlic in large bowl.
◊ In a small bowl, stir together vegetable oil, catsup, brown sugar, vinegar, salt, mustard and pepper. Pour over bean mixture and stir until beans are coated with sauce.
◊ Pour mixture into a 1 1/2-quart baking dish. Cover and bake at 350° F for about 1 hour.
◊ Remove cover and continue to cook for another 15 minutes, or until mixture is bubbling.

The Michigan Bean Commission
Leslie, Michigan

81

"TEX-MEX" STYLE POT ROAST
Yield: 6 servings

1 medium onion, chopped
1 tablespoon vegetable oil
2 to 3 pound beef chuck roast
1 (16 oz.) jar salsa
2 (4 oz. each) cans chopped green chilies, with liquid
1/2 teaspoon oregano
1/2 teaspoon salt
1/4 teaspoon pepper
1 (16 oz.) can chili beans
Chopped green onions
Shredded Cheddar or Monterey Jack cheese
Dairy sour cream

◊ Sauté chopped onion in vegetable oil in a large skillet until
  onions are tender. Remove onions from skillet and set aside.
◊ Trim visible fat from roast. Brown the roast slowly on both
  sides. Add onions, salsa, chilies, oregano, salt and pepper to
  the roast in the skillet. Cover and bake in a 350° F oven for 2
  hours.
◊ Remove meat from oven. Stir beans into salsa mixture. Baste
  meat with mixture. Cover and return to oven. Continue baking
  at 350° F for 30 minutes, or until roast is tender.
◊ Transfer meat and bean mixture to platter. Bean mixture may
  be served in a separate bowl if desired. Top each serving of
  meat with beans, chopped green onions, shredded cheese and
  sour cream.

82

GRAPES AND WINES

MAJOR GROWING AREAS

Michigan typically ranks about 5th in our nation for grape production each year. In the spring, cool breezes along the Lake Michigan shoreline help prevent the grapes from budding before danger of frost has passed. Grapes will not ripen after they have been picked from the vine, so allowing them ripen on the vine in the fall is very important. Moderate fall temperatures along the shoreline allow grapes to ripen on the vine before the first killing frost. Harvest generally starts in August and continues into early October. Once they are picked, the grapes are then cooled as quickly as possible to keep the quality high.

Most of the grapes grown in Michigan are Concords. They are used commercially to make some of the juices, jams and jellies available in the grocery store. Concord grapes may also be available at the local markets for making juice, jams, jellies and preserves at home.

Grapes for wine making are also grown in Michigan. Wineries can be found across the state. According to the Michigan Grape and Wine Industry Council, a wine is classified as a Michigan wine if at least 75% of the fruit is grown in Michigan. In addition to the grape wines pro-duced in the state, many of the other fruits readily available in Michigan are also used for making wine. (This chapter contains 2 recipes for peach wines.) The fruit wines will tend to be sweeter than grape wines. Several wineries now offer non-alcoholic wines and sparkling fruit juices in addition to their other wines.

STORING PRESERVES: Commercially prepared jams and jellies will keep well for up to 12 months. Jams and jellies should be refrigerated after opening.

WINE STORAGE: Store wines away from direct sunlight. A constant

83

temperature of 55° to 65° F is ideal. According to the Michigan Grape and Wine Industry Council, natural cork wines should be stored on their sides or upside down so the cork stays moist. If a wine is not properly stored, it may affect the quality of the wine. Check the label on the wine for other storage hints. Most Michigan wines are best used within a year or two of purchase.

Welch's has a plant in Lawton, Michigan that supplies Welch's grape juice, frozen concentrate and grape spreads for the central part of the United States. The Concord grapes for those products are grown in Michigan.

GRAND GRAPE GRANITE
Yield: 6, 6 oz. servings

12 ounces Welch's Purple Grape Juice
12 ounces lemon-lime soda
1/3 cup freshly squeezed lemon juice
Lemon twist

◊ Combine purple grape juice, soda, and lemon juice in large pitcher; stir well.
◊ Place in freezer for 2-4 hours, or until semi-frozen.
◊ Just before serving stir to break up the large ice crystals. The grape granite must always be liquid enough to be poured into a glass.

Welch's, Inc.
Concord, Massachusetts

For something really different, try this recipe. It does have a nice, strong grape flavor. If you prefer a milder grape taste, cut the amount of grape juice concentrate. Add one tablespoon water for each tablespoon of concentrate you omit from the recipe.

GRAPE CHIFFON PIE
Yield: 1, 9-inch pie

1 (.25 oz.) pkg. unflavored gelatin
1/2 cup water
1/4 cup sugar
1 (6 oz.) can frozen grape juice concentrate
2 tablespoons lemon juice
1 cup whipping cream
1 baked and cooled 9-inch graham cracker crust

◊ Combine gelatin, water and sugar in a saucepan. Let mixture sit for a few minutes to allow gelatin to soften. Heat on low heat until gelatin dissolves. Remove from heat. Add grape juice concentrate and lemon juice to gelatin and stir until concentrate is melted. Chill gelatin mixture for 10 to 15 minutes, or until mixture is syrupy.

◊ Beat whipping cream until soft peaks form. Fold gelatin mixture into whipped cream. Pour into prepared crust. Chill until firm.

FENN VALLEY GRILLED OR BAKED COD
Yield: 8 servings

1 cup Fenn Valley Seyval Blanc wine
2 tablespoons soy sauce
Juice from 1/2 lemon
2 green onions, chopped
1/4 teaspoon crushed tarragon
2 lbs. cod fillets
1 green pepper, sliced thin
1/2 lb. sliced mushrooms
1 onion, sliced thin
1 cup chopped fresh tomatoes
1/2 teaspoon ground oregano
1/4 teaspoon red pepper flakes
1/4 lb. feta cheese, crumbled

◊ To make marinade, mix together wine, soy sauce, lemon juice, chopped onions, and tarragon. Place cod in marinade and refrigerate for 2 hours. Do not use an aluminum pan, or marinade will have an off taste.
◊ Place fish on heavy foil if grilling, or a flat casserole pan if baking. Cover with sliced pepper, mushrooms, onion, tomatoes, oregano, pepper flakes and cheese. Wrap securely with the foil if grilling. Cover with foil to bake. Bake in preheated 350° oven for 30 minutes, or place on hot grill for about 20 minutes.
◊ Serve with Fenn Valley Seyval Blanc. This is a very flavorful way to serve fish for health and diet conscious people.

Ruth Welsch
Fenn Valley Vineyards
Fennville, Michigan

THE NATURAL WARMER
Yield: 1 serving

4 oz. (1/2 cup) Naturally Old Fashioned® Peach Wine
Dash of ground allspice, cinnamon, or cloves
1 teaspoon honey

◊ Pour wine into a microwave-safe mug or glass. Add dash of
  allspice, cinnamon, or cloves, as desired. Cook on high power
  in microwave oven for 1 to 1 1/4 minutes, or until warm.
◊ Stir in honey. Serve immediately.
◊ NOTE: Whole allspice, cinnamon or honey may be added to
  the wine in the bottle. Allow time for the flavors to blend before
  heating as described above.

Peterson and Sons Winery
Kalamazoo, Michigan

THE NATURAL COOLER
Yield: 1 serving

4 oz. (1/2 cup) Naturally Old Fashioned® Rhubarb-Raspberry
  Wine
4 oz. (1/2 cup) lemon-lime soda pop (such as Squirt® or
  Slice®)
Ice

◊ Mix together wine and soda pop. Pour over lots of ice in a tall
  glass. Serve immediately.

Peterson and Sons Winery
Kalamazoo, Michigan

87

PEACH ALEXANDER
Yield: 4 to 6 servings

1 medium fresh peach (canned or frozen peach may also be used)
1 pint vanilla ice cream
4 to 6 ounces St. Julian Peach Wine*

◊ Peel and chop peach. Place ice cream, peach wine and chopped peach in blender. Process until smooth. Serve immediately.
◊ *HINT: Non-alcoholic peach wine may also be used.

Wilma Williams
St. Julian Winery
Paw Paw

MAY WINE SLUSH
Yield: 10 to 15 servings

2 cups St. Julian May Wine
1 pint strawberries
1 (6 oz.) can frozen lemonade concentrate
8 - 10 ice cubes

◊ Combine wine, strawberries, lemonade concentrate and ice cubes in blender. Process until smooth. Serve immediately.
◊ HINT: May also be frozen.

Wilma Williams
St. Julian Winery
Paw Paw

88

GREEN BEANS

MAJOR GROWING AREAS

Look for freshly harvested Michigan green beans starting in mid-July. The harvest continues on into early October. While some green beans are grown commercially for fresh market sales, most are commercially canned and some are frozen. Michigan typically ranks 4th in the nation for production of green beans for processing. Michigan grown green beans are shipped across the United States.

When choosing fresh green beans, make sure the beans are crisp and tender. A fresh bean should snap in half cleanly. To prepare beans before cooking, wash the beans and snap off both tips. The beans may then be snapped into smaller pieces, if desired. For best flavor, green beans should be blanched before being frozen. Pressure canning is the only safe method for canning beans.

Green beans have very few calories, yet they supply iron, potassium, Vitamin A, and Vitamin C to our diets. Green beans are a good source of fiber.

HOW MUCH TO BUY??? One pound of fresh green beans will be 2 to 3 cups of beans. Generally, one pound of fresh green beans will serve four people.

SELECTION: Choose green beans which look fresh and have good color. Select young, unblemished, tender pods which are firm and crisp.

AVOID: Thick and tough green beans are overmature and should be avoided. Do not choose beans which are wilted, blemished or show signs of decay.

STORAGE: Wash beans and pat dry before refrigerating. The extra moisture will help prevent the beans from drying out. Store green beans in a plastic bag in the crisper section of the refrigerator.

89

SAUCY GREEN BEANS
Yield: 4 servings

1 tablespoon butter or margarine, melted
1/4 cup dairy sour cream
1 tablespoon catsup
1 teaspoon Worcestershire sauce
1/8 teaspoon ground pepper
1 (10 oz.) pkg. frozen French-cut green beans

◊ In a small bowl, stir together butter, sour cream, catsup,
  Worcestershire sauce and pepper. Set aside.
◊ Cook green beans according to package directions. Drain
  water from beans. Immediately pour sour cream sauce over
  beans. Stir gently until beans are coated with sauce. Serve
  immediately.

FRESH GREEN BEAN SALAD
Yield: 4 servings

1 pound green beans (young and tender are best)
1 bunch green onions, sliced
1 teaspoon dill sauce
2 tablespoons olive oil or vegetable oil
2 tablespoons red wine vinegar
1 teaspoon Dijon mustard
1/4 teaspoon ground black pepper

◊ Snap beans into bite-size pieces. Cook in small amount of
  boiling water until crisp-tender (about 5-8 minutes). Drain
  water from beans. Run cool water over beans to prevent
  further cooking.
◊ Transfer beans to serving dish and stir in sliced green onions.
◊ In a small bowl, whisk together dill sauce, oil, vinegar, mustard
  and pepper until blended. Pour over beans. Toss lightly.
  Serve.

GREEN BEAN-TOMATO SAUTÉ
Yield: 2 servings

1 cup snapped fresh green beans (about 1/2 pound beans)
Water
1 tablespoon vegetable oil
1 tablespoon butter or margarine
1 cup cherry tomatoes, halved
2 tablespoons chopped ham
1 teaspoon soy sauce
Fresh ground black pepper, to taste

◊ Cook beans in boiling water for 3 to 4 minutes, or until crisp-tender. (Beans may also be cooked in the microwave. Cook, covered, on high power for 3 minutes with 1 tablespoon water until crisp-tender.) Drain.

◊ Heat oil and butter in medium skillet. Add beans, tomatoes and ham. Cook over medium heat, stirring often, for about 2 minutes. Add soy sauce and continue cooking for 1 more minute, or until heated through. Season with pepper. Serve immediately.

GREEN BEANS

MICROWAVE GREEN BEANS WITH PEPPER BUTTER
Yield: 4 servings

2 tablespoons butter or margarine
1/3 cup finely chopped green pepper
1 tablespoon chopped green onion
1 teaspoon lemon juice
1/4 teaspoon salt
1/8 teaspoon paprika
1 (15 1/2 oz.) can green beans, drained

◊ In a 1-quart microwave safe casserole dish, combine butter, green pepper, green onion, lemon juice, salt and paprika. Cover and cook on high power for 1 1/2 to 3 minutes, or until vegetables are tender.
◊ Process cooked vegetables and seasonings in a food processor or blender until smooth. Return to casserole dish. Add drained beans and stir until mixed.
◊ Cover and cook on high power for 2 to 4 minutes, or until beans are heated through. Stir once during cooking time.

SAVORY GREEN BEANS AND POTATOES
Yield: 6 servings

1 (14.5 oz.) can chicken broth
1 (10 oz.) pkg. frozen green beans
4 medium potatoes
3 slices bacon, cooked and crumbled
Pepper

◊ In a medium saucepan, combine chicken broth and green beans. Cut potatoes into large chunks and add to green bean mixture. Stir in bacon.
◊ Simmer over low heat for 35 to 45 minutes, or until vegetables are tender and flavors are blended.
◊ NOTE: This mixture tastes better each time it is reheated, so plan to make leftovers. Potatoes may be used with or without skin, depending on your preference. New potatoes may be used with great results.

92

HONEY

The approximately 80,000 honey bee colonies in the state of Michigan produce over 5 million pounds of honey each year. For the fruit farmers in the state, the pollination of blossoms for the fruit crop done by the honey bees is crucial. As the honey bees are busy collecting nectar, they help carry pollen among flower blossoms. Once pollinated, the blossoms mature into fruit.

Naturally sweet honey is produced by the honey bees from the nectar they gather from various plants. The flavor and color of a given honey depend on the nectar the bees used to make it. Some commercially packed honeys are blended to maintain a standard flavor and color. According to the Michigan Bee Keepers Association, the first honeys of the season in Michigan are usually light in color with a mild flavor. Harvest generally begins in mid-July. In the fall, harvest continues through October. By now the honeys have a stronger flavor and the color has deepened to an amber color.

It is natural for honey to granulate (or crystallize) during storage. To liquify the honey again, place the container of honey in a pan of warm (not hot) water. Let it remain in the water until it becomes clear again. Honey should be stored in a covered container at room temperature.

HOW MUCH TO BUY??? A 12-ounce (by weight) jar equals 1, 8-ounce measuring cup of liquid.

SELECTION: The lighter colored honeys have a mild flavor, while the darker amber honeys have a stronger flavor. Choosing the best flavor is a matter of personal preference.

STORAGE: Store honey in an air-tight container at room temperature.

HONEY OATMEAL BREAD
Yield: 2 loaves

1 cup quick cooking oats
1/2 cup whole wheat flour
1/2 cup honey
2 teaspoons salt
2 tablespoons butter or margarine
2 cups boiling water
1 (1/4 oz.) package active dry yeast
1/2 cup lukewarm water
5 cups all-purpose flour

◊ Place oats, whole wheat flour, honey, salt and butter in large bowl. Pour boiling water over mixture and stir until well blended. Set aside until mixture is cooled to lukewarm.

◊ Dissolve yeast in 1/2 cup warm water. Add to oat mixture. Stir in 5 cups all-purpose flour. Turn dough out onto lightly floured board. Knead 5-10 minutes, or until dough is smooth and elastic. Place in greased bowl, cover, and let rise until doubled (about 45 minutes).

◊ Punch down dough. Let rest for 10 minutes. Shape into 2 loaves and place in greased 9 x 5 x 3-inch pans. Let rise until doubled (about 30 minutes).

◊ Bake in **preheated 375°** oven for 40 - 45 minutes. Cool in pan for 5 minutes. Remove from pan and cool on wire rack.

94

HONEY PUMPKIN PIE
Yield: 1, 9-inch pie

1 (1 lb.) can pumpkin
1/2 cup honey
1/2 cup brown sugar, firmly packed
1 tablespoon cornstarch
1 teaspoon ground cinnamon
1 teaspoon ground nutmeg
1/2 teaspoon salt
1 1/2 cups milk
2 eggs
2 tablespoons butter or margarine, melted
1, 9-inch unbaked pie crust, with fluted edge to hold large
   filling

◊ Preheat oven to 400° F.
◊ In a large bowl, combine pumpkin, honey, brown sugar,
   cornstarch, cinnamon, nutmeg, and salt. Stir in milk, eggs,
   and melted butter. Pour into prepared pie crust.
◊ Bake at 400° for 60 to 65 minutes, or until a knife inserted
   halfway between outer edge and center comes out clean.

95

HONEY AND MUSTARD GLAZED CHICKEN
Yield: 4 to 6 servings

1/4 cup butter or margarine
1/2 cup honey
1/4 cup prepared mustard
1 tablespoon soy sauce
1 teaspoon lemon juice
1/2 teaspoon salt
1 (3 to 4 lb.) frying chicken, cut-up

◊ Preheat oven to 375° F.
◊ Melt butter or margarine. Add honey, mustard, soy sauce, lemon juice, and salt. Whisk together until smooth.
◊ Pour honey mixture into a greased shallow baking pan. Roll each piece of chicken in honey mixture and place in baking pan meat-side-up.
◊ Bake at 375° for 50 to 60 minutes, or until chicken is thoroughly cooked and tender.

HONEY BUTTER
Yield: 3/4 cup

1/2 cup (1 stick) butter or margarine, softened
1/3 cup honey
1 teaspoon orange juice

◊ Beat together butter, honey and orange juice until smooth and creamy.
◊ Store in a covered container in the refrigerator.
◊ NOTE: Tastes great on pancakes, muffins, toast, bread, and biscuits.

The honey in these cookies helps them to stay moist.

PEANUT BUTTER AND HONEY COOKIES
Yield: 3 dozen cookies

1/2 cup shortening
1/2 cup brown sugar, firmly packed
1/2 cup honey
1/2 cup peanut butter
1 egg
1 1/2 cups all-purpose flour
1/2 teaspoon baking soda
1/2 teaspoon salt
1/2 teaspoon ground nutmeg

◊ Preheat oven to 375° F.
◊ Beat together the shortening, brown sugar, honey, peanut butter and egg until smooth and creamy.
◊ In a small bowl, stir together the flour, baking soda, salt and nutmeg. Stir flour mixture into the creamed honey mixture.
◊ Drop the dough by teaspoonfuls onto an ungreased cookie sheet. Bake in 375° oven for 8 to 10 minutes, or until set and lightly brown around the edges. Let stand 3 to 5 minutes before removing from cookie sheet to cooling rack.

CORNMEAL MUFFINS
Yield: 12 muffins

1 1/2 cups all-purpose flour
2 teaspoons baking powder
1/4 teaspoon baking soda
3/4 teaspoon salt
3/4 cup yellow cornmeal
1 egg
3 tablespoons honey
4 tablespoons vegetable oil
1 cup milk

◊ Preheat oven to 425° F.
◊ Sift flour once, measure, add baking powder, baking soda and salt. Sift again, then mix in cornmeal.
◊ Combine egg, honey, oil and milk and add to dry ingredients, stirring only enough to dampen all flour. Spoon into well-greased muffin pans and bake at 425° for 25 minutes, or until golden brown.

Gerry Buell
Michigan Beekeepers Association
Milford, Michigan

MAPLE SYRUP

Pancakes have never tasted better than with a topping of pure Michigan maple syrup. More than 80,000 gallons of syrup are produced in Michigan each year. Michigan usually ranks fifth or higher nationally for syrup production. Many fruit and vegetable stands across the state sell pure maple syrup. Maple syrup can also be purchased year round from most of the "sugar shacks" that produce maple syrup in Michigan.

Collection of sap from the maple trees starts in late winter when the days start to become warm and sunny, but the nights still have freezing temperatures. A tree must have at least a 10-inch diameter before it can safely be tapped. This means that the tree is usually 30 to 40 years old before it can be tapped. As the diameter of the tree becomes larger, more taps can be added. The sap flows from the tree through the tap and into some type of container. Sap is pumped through the entire tree and the tap only affects the flow of sap right around the tap. Each year the taps are moved 6 - 12" for the health of the tree.

It does take about 40 gallons of sap to produce 1 gallon of maple syrup. The extra moisture in the sap is boiled off to concentrate the sugars and flavor. The pure maple syrup is then bottled or canned. Maple syrup which has been processed this way can be stored on the shelf until you are ready to open the container. An opened container of maple syrup should be stored in the refrigerator.

In Michigan's Upper Peninsula, Scott and Elise Bunce of the Rock River Sugar Bush in Chatham sometimes wade through 4 feet of snow to start tapping maple syrup in late February. The snow is gone and spring is here when they finish up in April. They suggest you try maple syrup for glazing ham, as a topping for ice cream or even as a sweetener for coffee!

99

If you like pecan pie, you're sure to love this rich maple dessert.

MAPLE PECAN SQUARES
Yield: 9 servings

Crust:
1/2 cup melted butter
1/4 cup brown sugar, firmly packed
1 cup all-purpose flour

Topping:
2/3 cup brown sugar, firmly packed
1 cup pure maple syrup
1/4 cup butter
2 eggs, slightly beaten
1/8 teaspoon salt
2/3 cup chopped pecans
1/2 teaspoon vanilla
2 tablespoons all-purpose flour
Ice cream or whipped topping (optional)

◊ Preheat oven to 350° F.
◊ Place melted butter, 1/4 cup brown sugar and flour in 8 x 8-inch baking pan. Stir together with fork or fingers. Press onto bottom of pan. Bake at 350° for 5 minutes. Set aside. Preheat oven to 400° F.
◊ For topping, combine 2/3 cup brown sugar and maple syrup in pan. Simmer over low heat for 5 minutes. Cool to lukewarm. Stir in butter until melted. Stir in beaten eggs. Add salt, pecans, vanilla and flour. Stir until well-mixed. Pour over partially baked crust. Bake in preheated 400° oven for 5 minutes. Reduce heat to 350° and continue baking for 20 minutes, or until bubbling. Serve with ice cream or whipped topping.

Livingston Farms
St. Johns, Michigan

100

Squash is plentiful at Michigan farm markets in the fall. The microwave oven is a real time saver when cooking squash.

MICROWAVED MAPLE SQUASH
Yield: 2 servings

1 acorn squash
1/4 cup butter or margarine
1/4 cup pure maple syrup
Chopped pecans or raisins

◊ Cut acorn squash in half lengthwise, remove seeds. Place both halves in shallow microwave dish. Sprinkle with water. Cover loosely with plastic wrap and cook on high power for 9 to 11 minutes, or until squash is tender.
◊ When squash is cool enough to handle, scoop out the flesh and place in bowl. Mash squash with potato masher or fork. Stir in butter and maple syrup until butter is melted. Spread mixture in 1-quart microwave dish or spoon back into squash shells. Garnish squash mixture with pecans or raisins. Cover loosely with plastic wrap and cook on high power for 2 to 4 minutes, or until heated through.

This maple syrup dressing is for topping fruit salads. The folks at Livingston Farms also note that it is delicious on apple or peach cobblers, plain warm sponge cake, steamed pudding or plain rice. We tried it on Cherry Kuchen (check index) - what a treat!

MAPLE SYRUP DRESSING
Yield: 3 cups

1/4 cup lemon juice
1/4 cup orange juice
1/4 cup pineapple juice
1/2 cup pure maple syrup
2 egg whites, stiffly beaten
1/2 cup heavy cream
2 tablespoons sugar

◊ In a double boiler combine lemon, orange and pineapple juices plus maple syrup. Cook until like a thin custard, stirring constantly. Remove from heat and fold in beaten egg whites. Chill.
◊ Just before serving, beat together cream and sugar until stiff peaks form. Fold whipped cream into maple syrup mixture.

Livingston Farms
St. Johns, Michigan

MAPLE APPLESAUCE MUFFINS
Yield: 18 muffins

2 cups all-purpose flour
1 tablespoon baking powder
1 teaspoon salt
1/2 teaspoon ground cinnamon
1/2 cup shortening
1/4 cup sugar
3/4 cup pure maple syrup
2 eggs
3/4 cup applesauce

◊ Preheat oven to 375° F.
◊ Stir together flour, baking powder, salt and cinnamon. Set aside.
◊ Cream shortening and sugar until fluffy. Add maple syrup. Stir in eggs and applesauce. Mixture tends to curdle. Stir in set aside flour mixture. Fill greased muffin cups 2/3 full. Bake at 375° for 20 minutes, or until golden brown.

Dodd's Sugar Shack
Niles, Michigan

MAPLE FLAVORED FROSTING
Yield: about 1 1/4 cups frosting

2 tablespoons butter or margarine, softened
1/4 cup pure maple syrup
2 tablespoons milk
2 cups powdered sugar

◊ In a medium mixing bowl, cream butter until smooth. Combine
  maple syrup and milk. Add one-half of maple syrup mixture
  and one-half powdered sugar to butter and beat until smooth.
  Add remaining maple syrup mixture and powdered sugar;
  continue beating until smooth and creamy.
◊ HINT: More powdered sugar or maple syrup may be added if
  necessary to achieve the consistency you desire.

*Dodd's Sugar Shack in Niles, Michigan offers the
following ideas for using the darker grades of syrup:*

* As a glaze for baked carrots, squash or sweet
  potatoes.
* As a glaze for broiled or baked fruit, such as baked
  apples and bananas, or broiled grapefruit, pineapple
  slices.
* As a sauce for apple or peach dumplings.
* To sweeten milk shakes or eggnogs.
* As a sauce for puddings and custards.

MUSHROOMS

Michigan produces over 20 million pounds of mushrooms a year, making our state the third largest mushroom producer in this country. Mushrooms are difficult to grow commercially and require very special growing conditions. To achieve these special growing conditions, mushrooms are grown in darkness in indoor bedding buildings. Since they are grown in these special conditions, mushrooms are available for us to enjoy year round.

For wild mushroom lovers, Michigan is also a good place to hunt for morel mushrooms. These cone-shaped mushrooms have a nut-like taste.

Use mushrooms as quickly as possible for freshest flavor. Wash mushrooms gently before using them, especially wild mushrooms which may be sandy. Don't let mushrooms soak in water though, or they will become waterlogged.

HOW MUCH TO BUY??? One pound of mushrooms will serve 3 to 4 people and will make 4 to 5 cups of sliced mushrooms (before cooking).

SELECTION: Choose mushrooms with a solid color (it may be white to light brown, depending on the mushroom). Look for tight fitting caps. As mushrooms age and moisture is lost, the caps pull away from the stems. Go ahead and use older mushrooms as long as they are dry and show no signs of decay.

AVOID: Discolored, decayed or blemished mushrooms should be avoided. Overripe mushrooms with dark, discolored gills under the cap should be discarded.

STORAGE: Refrigerate mushrooms in a paper bag or open container. Cover mushrooms loosely with a damp paper towel. Mushrooms should not be washed until just before they are used. Never let them soak in water. Mushrooms will store well in the refrigerator for up to a week.

This sauce works well over many meats. Try serving it over meatloaf, roast beef or even hamburgers!

MUSHROOM SAUCE
Yield: 1 cup sauce

1 cup sliced fresh mushrooms
2 tablespoons butter or margarine
2 teaspoons cornstarch
1/2 teaspoon lemon juice
Dash Tabasco sauce
1 beef flavored bouillon cube
3/4 cup boiling water

◊ Sauté mushrooms in butter until tender. Remove from heat.
◊ Mix cornstarch with a small amount of cold water until dissolved. Stir in lemon juice and Tabasco sauce. Add to mushrooms.
◊ Combine bouillon cube and boiling water. Stir until bouillon cube is dissolved. Add to mushroom mixture. Return to heat and continue to cook, stirring often, until mixture is thickened. Serve immediately.
◊ NOTE: Mushrooms may be sliced or chopped depending on your personal preference.

MARINATED MUSHROOMS
Yield: 8 servings

1 (12 oz.) pkg. fresh mushrooms (about 1 1/2 cups)
1/2 cup olive oil
1/4 cup lemon juice
1 bunch green onions, sliced
2 teaspoons dried parsley, or 4 sprigs fresh parsley,
  snipped
1 teaspoon Worcestershire sauce
1/8 teaspoon red cayenne pepper
1 teaspoon garlic salt

◊ Clean mushrooms. Place in shallow dish.
◊ Whisk together olive oil, lemon juice, sliced onions, parsley,
  Worcestershire sauce, cayenne pepper and garlic salt. Pour
  over mushrooms. Stir until all mushrooms have been coated
  with dressing. Cover and refrigerate several hours (or overnight) stirring occasionally. Serve with decorative toothpicks.

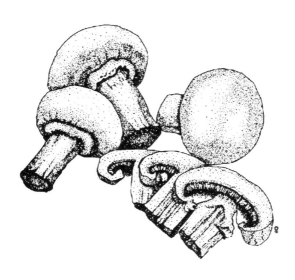

LEMON BROILED SCALLOPS AND MUSHROOMS
Yield: 2-3 servings

1/4 cup lemon juice
2 tablespoons Teriyaki sauce
2 tablespoons vegetable oil
1 clove garlic, crushed
1/2 teaspoon salt
1/4 teaspoon paprika
1/4 teaspoon ground black pepper
1 pound sea scallops
1 (8 oz.) pkg. mushrooms, cleaned and trimmed
Lemon wedges for garnish

◊ In a large bowl, whisk together lemon juice, Teriyaki sauce, oil, garlic, salt, paprika and pepper. Add the scallops and mushrooms and coat well. Cover and marinate in refrigerator for 1 to 3 hours, turning occasionally.
◊ Using a slotted spoon, transfer scallops and mushrooms to a lightly oiled broiler pan. Broil 5 inches from heat for 4 minutes. Turn mushrooms and scallops over, brush with marinade and broil 4 more minutes, or until cooked through. If mushrooms cook too quickly, remove them from broiler pan during last few minutes of cooking.
◊ Garnish with lemon wedges and serve immediately.

Most people look shocked when I mention a recipe for a mushroom ice cream topping. Give it a try though, the sauce really is good! The tender mushrooms blend well with the pecans and sweet syrup.

PHILLIPS MILL MARVELOUS MOREL SUNDAE
Yield: 4 servings

3 tablespoons butter
1 cup morels, finely chopped
1 tablespoon honey
1/4 cup chopped pecans
1/2 cup butter, melted
1 cup brown sugar, firmly packed
Juice from 1/4 lemon
1/4 cup Frangelico liqueur
Vernors Flavored ice cream (or vanilla)

◊ Sauté the morels in 3 tablespoons of butter. Mix in the honey and pecans.
◊ Stir together 1/2 cup melted butter, brown sugar, lemon juice and Frangelico. Add this to the pecan and morel mixture.
◊ Serve warm over Vernors Flavored ice cream.
◊ This topping is also good on most any ice cream, cheesecake, cake and lots of other desserts, including fresh fruit.
◊ NOTE: Other mushrooms, such as button mushrooms found in the grocery store may be substituted for the morels.

Dave and Gale Phillips
Wharfside
Charlevoix, Michigan

SIMPLY DELICIOUS MUSHROOM APPETIZERS
Yield: 4 servings

1 (3 oz.) pkg. cream cheese
1 tablespoon real bacon bits
1 tablespoon chopped green onion
1 (8 oz.) pkg. fresh mushrooms
Paprika

◊ Preheat oven to 350° F.
◊ In a small bowl, beat cream cheese until smooth. Stir in bacon bits and green onion.
◊ Clean mushrooms. Remove stem from each mushroom and set aside for use in another recipe or for salad.
◊ Spread cheese filling in each mushroom. Divide filling among all mushrooms. Place mushrooms in shallow baking pan with the filling side up.
◊ Sprinkle paprika over mushrooms. Bake at 350° for 20 minutes, or until mushrooms are tender and juicy. Serve immediately.

ONIONS

According to the Michigan Onion
Committee, the majority of
Michigan's onion crop is a
pungent cooking onion which
can be held in storage from
harvest (September) until the
end of March or later. The
onions are shipped from storage
through the autumn and winter
seasons.   The thick, dark outer skin sets this onion apart from fresh
onions. The skin on the storage onion protects it during shipping.
These onions are sold in 2, 3 and 5 pound bags. Most Michigan onions
are grown in organic "muck" soils.

MAJOR GROWING AREAS

Don't judge an onion by it's size or color. Size does not determine
quality or flavor. The seed used, the soil and weather during the
growing season help determine how mild or pungent an onion will be.

It is easy to freeze onions to be used later in casseroles, soups or other
cooked dishes. Peel and chop as many onions as desired. Spread
them out on a single layer on a cookie sheet. Cover them with a vapor
proof wrap (this keeps the freezer from smelling strongly of onions).
When frozen, transfer the chopped onion to a freezer storage bag.
When the recipe calls for chopped onions, pour out as many as you
need. The onions will soften in texture by being frozen this way, so they
are best used in cooked dishes.

HOW MUCH TO BUY??? Buy 1 large, 2 medium or 3-4 small onions
per serving. One pound is usually equal to 3 medium onions.

SELECTION: When selecting storage onions, look for onions that are
firm or hard and well-shaped. Look for onions with a short neck and
dry, paperlike skin. The quality of the onion is not affected by its size.

AVOID: Check the neck on the onion . Avoid those with a wet, soggy
feeling at the neck . Onions which are sprouting and those with many
spots or blemishes should be avoided.

111

ONIONS

STORAGE: Store onions in the refrigerator or in a cool room (around 50 to 60 is best). Always keep them dry and well ventilated in a dark area away from the sun. They can be stored for weeks, but should be used before they soften or sprout. Spread the onions out in a single layer for longer storage. Onions should never be stored with potatoes because they will take on moisture from the potatoes and decay quickly.

SAUTÉED ONIONS FOR HAMBURGERS
Yield: 4 servings

1 or 2 whole Michigan onions
2 tablespoons butter or margarine
Salt (optional)

◊ Peel and slice onions.
◊ Melt butter or margarine in skillet. Fry onions in butter over medium heat until golden brown. Add salt to taste.
◊ Cover skillet, reduce heat and simmer onions until tender, stirring occasionally.
◊ NOTE : The onions add terrific flavor to meat when served over hamburgers or steaks.

Maynard Klamer
President, Michigan Onion Committee
Byron Center, Michigan

The wonderful smell of the onions as they are being sautéed will have everyone asking "When do we eat?" The Swiss cheese adds just the right subtle flavor to the onions.

RICE-ONION-CHEESE CASSEROLE
Yield: 4 to 6 servings

3 tablespoons butter or margarine
4 medium onions, peeled and cut into chunks
1 cup cooked rice
1/2 teaspoon salt
1/2 cup (2 oz.) shredded Swiss cheese
1/2 cup half-and-half or heavy cream

◊ Preheat oven to 325° F.
◊ In large skillet, melt butter over medium heat. Add onions and sauté until transparent. Remove from heat.
◊ Add cooked rice, salt, cheese and cream to onions and mix well.
◊ Place mixture in greased, 2-quart shallow baking dish.
◊ Bake at 325° for 40 to 45 minutes, or until heated through.

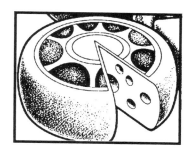

ONION SOUP
Yield: 3 servings

1 tablespoon margarine, melted
1 tablespoon vegetable oil
2 medium onions, sliced
1/8 teaspoon sugar
2 teaspoons all-purpose flour
2 1/2 cups water
2 unsalted beef bouillon cubes
2 tablespoons vermouth or dry white table wine
1/8 teaspoon pepper
1 slice bread, toasted and cut into cubes

◊ Combine margarine, oil and onions in pan. Cover and cook over low heat for 15 minutes.
◊ Add sugar and cook uncovered 10 minutes, stirring occasionally, until the onions are a deep golden brown.
◊ Mix in flour. Stir in water. Add bouillon cubes, vermouth and pepper and simmer 15 - 30 minutes.
◊ Place soup in cup and top with cubes of toast.

Michigan Onion Committee
Hudsonville, Michigan

This is an especially tasty mixture. The recipe calls for sliced French Bread, but it is just as good on crackers or melba toast.

ONION PÂTÉ
Yield: approximately 1 2/3 cup paté

1/2 cup chopped onion
1 (8 oz.) package fresh mushrooms, cleaned and chopped
1 tablespoon vegetable oil
2 (3 oz. each) packages cream cheese, quartered
1/4 cup grated Parmesan cheese
1/4 cup minced fresh parsley
2 tablespoons soy sauce
French Bread, thinly sliced

◊ Sauté onions and mushrooms in hot oil in large skillet over medium heat 2 minutes; remove from heat.
◊ Stir in cream cheese until blended. Add Parmesan cheese, parsley and soy sauce, stirring to combine.
◊ Refrigerate, covered, 3 hours, or until thoroughly chilled. Serve with French bread slices.

Michigan Onion Committee
Hudsonville, Michigan

115

CHEESY VEGETABLE SOUP
Yield: 4 servings

1 cup peeled, diced potatoes
1 cup chopped onion
1/2 cup sliced carrots
1/2 cup chopped celery
1 1/2 cups water
3 chicken flavored bouillon cubes
1 cup milk
1/4 cup cornstarch
1 1/2 cups (6 oz.) shredded Cheddar cheese
1/2 teaspoon dry mustard
Dash cayenne pepper

◊ In a 4-quart saucepan, combine potatoes, chopped onion, carrots, celery, water and bouillon cubes. Bring to a boil. Reduce heat, cover and simmer 30 minutes or until vegetables are tender.
◊ In a small bowl, combine milk and cornstarch; stir until smooth. Gradually blend into vegetable mixture.
◊ Add cheese, mustard and pepper. Continue to heat and stir until mixture becomes very hot and thickened. Do not allow mixture to boil. Serve immediately.

Suggested Menu

Cheesy Vegetable Soup
Turkey Salad Submarines
Purple Plum Tart

116

PEACHES

In Michigan we are fortunate to have fresh peaches available from July to late September. Many people look forward to early August when the Red Haven peaches become ripe. Michigan typically ranks about 6th in the United States for

MAJOR GROWING AREAS

peach production. Most Michigan peaches are sold as fresh peaches, although some are commercially canned or frozen. The majority of Michigan peaches are free-stone, which means the pit will separate easily from the flesh when the peaches are ripe.

Fresh, juicy peaches are a treat eaten out of hand. Peaches may also be frozen or canned. While many peaches need ascorbic acid to prevent browning when freezing, Michigan developed "haven" varieties (except for the Halehaven peach) are resistant to browning.

HOW MUCH TO BUY??? 1 pound is generally 3 medium peaches and will yield 2 cups of sliced peaches. Allow 1 peach per serving.

SELECTION: Look for firm, well-formed fruit which is free from decay and bruising. A ripe peach should have a golden or creamy yellow background color, and that wonderful "peach" smell.

AVOID: A peach with a green background color was picked too early and the immature fruit will lack flavor and never ripen properly. Avoid peaches with shriveled skin and those which are too soft and overripe.

STORAGE: Most peaches are picked at the firm-ripe stage and may need to ripen a few days to soften and become fully ripe. For best results, ripen peaches at room temperature away from sunlight, in a loosely closed paper bag or ripening bowl. Fully ripened peaches should be refrigerated and used within one or two weeks.

PEACHES AND CREAM CHEESECAKE
Yield: 1, 9" cheesecake

Crust:
1 1/4 cups all-purpose flour
1/3 cup butter or margarine
1/4 cup egg yolk (about 3 yolks), slightly beaten

Cheesecake:
4 (8 oz. each) pkgs. cream cheese
1 1/4 cups sugar
4 large eggs, slightly beaten
1/2 cup heavy cream
1 teaspoon vanilla
1 cup fresh, ripe, Michigan peach slices
1 tablespoon sugar
Fresh or canned Michigan peaches

◊ Preheat oven to 300° F.
◊ To prepare crust, place flour in mixing bowl. Cut in butter until crumbly. Stir in egg yolks. Place mixture in a 9-inch springform pan. With a spoon, press crust over bottom of pan and 1/2 inch up the sides of the pan. Set aside.
◊ Beat cream cheese and 1 1 /4 cups sugar together until smooth. Add eggs, cream and vanilla. Beat until well mixed. Pour into prepared crust.
◊ Place 1 cup peaches and 1 tablespoon sugar in food processor or blender. Process for 20 seconds, or until smooth. Swirl puréed peaches through cream cheese mixture.
◊ Bake in 300° oven for 1 hour and 35 minutes. Turn off oven and leave cake in oven for another hour. Cool on a rack to room temperature. Chill. Garnish with thin slices of fresh or canned Michigan peaches.

Marian Sheridan
The Gourmet Cheesecake Club
Farmington Hills, Michigan

PEACH POPS
Yield: 6 pops

4 fresh peaches
1/3 cup orange juice concentrate
1/4 cup sugar

◊ Peel and slice peaches. Place in food processor or blender.
  Add orange juice concentrate and sugar. Process until smooth.
◊ Pour mixture into popcicle forms or small paper cups with
  sticks inserted for handles. Freeze until solid. Enjoy.

Jerry Jollay
Michigan Peach Sponsors
Coloma, Michigan

BERRY AND PEACH GELATIN SALAD
Yield: 5 to 6 servings

1 (3 oz.) pkg. peach flavored gelatin
1 cup hot water
1/8 teaspoon ground cinnamon
1 cup apple juice
2 1/2 cups sliced peaches
1 cup berries (blueberries, raspberries, strawberries or
  blackberries may be used)

◊ In a 1 1/2-quart bowl combine gelatin and hot water. Stir until
  gelatin is dissolved.
◊ Stir in cinnamon and apple juice. Stir in peaches and berries.
  Cover and refrigerate until mixture is set.

119

PEACH MUFFINS
Yield: 12 muffins

2 cups all-purpose flour
1/2 teaspoon salt
2 1/2 teaspoons baking powder
1/4 cup sugar
1 cup milk
1 egg, slightly beaten
1/4 cup melted shortening
3/4 cup chopped canned peaches, well drained
2 tablespoons sugar
1 teaspoon ground cinnamon
1/2 teaspoon ground nutmeg

◊ Preheat oven to 400° F.
◊ Sift together flour, salt, baking powder and 1/4 cup sugar.
  Combine milk, egg and shortening; stir quickly into dry ingredients. Fold in peaches. Turn into well greased muffin pans,
  filling 2/3 full.
◊ Mix 2 tablespoons sugar, cinnamon and nutmeg together and
  sprinkle over muffins.
◊ Bake in 400° oven for 25 minutes, or until top springs back
  when lightly pressed with finger.

Jerry Jollay
Michigan Peach Sponsors
Coloma, Michigan

CHIFFON PEACH PIE
Yield: 1, 9-inch pie

3 to 4 fresh, ripe peaches*
1 tablespoon lemon juice
1 (1/4 oz.) envelope unflavored gelatin
1/2 cup sugar
2 tablespoons orange flavored liqueur
1 cup whipping cream
1 baked, cooled 9-inch pie shell
Whipped cream, peach slices for garnish

◊ Peel and dice peaches. Process peaches in food processor or blender until puréed. (You should have about 2 cups of purée.)
◊ Combine 1/2 cup of the purée with lemon juice in small saucepan and sprinkle with gelatin. Let stand 5 minutes to soften gelatin.
◊ Set small saucepan of gelatin mixture in larger pan of hot water and heat, stirring constantly until gelatin dissolves. (See NOTE below.) Stir in remaining puréed peach, sugar and orange flavored liqueur. Cool until mixture begins to thicken.
◊ Beat cream until stiff. Fold into gelatin mixture. Chill until mixture mounds on spoon. Turn into pie shell and chill until firm, at least 4 hours.
◊ If desired, garnish pie with small mounds of whipped cream and peach slices just before serving.

* 1 (16 oz.) package frozen peaches may be substituted for fresh peaches. Partially defrost peaches before using.

◊ NOTE: Peach purée and gelatin may be heated in the microwave instead of in a saucepan. Use a small, microwave safe container and heat on half power for 3 to 4 minutes, or until gelatin is dissolved.

PEACH CRUMBLE
Yield: 9 servings

Crust:
2 1/2 cups all-purpose flour
1 tablespoon sugar
1 teaspoon salt
3/4 cup vegetable oil
3 tablespoons milk

Filling:
1 cup sugar
3 tablespoons all-purpose flour
1 tablespoon lemon juice
1/4 teaspoon ground cinnamon
Dash salt
4 cups sliced peaches

◊ Preheat oven to 450° F.
◊ Mix together 2 1/2 cups flour, 1 tablespoon sugar, salt, oil, and milk until blended. Set aside 1/3 of crust mixture.
◊ Pat remaining 2/3 of crust mixture into bottom and 1-inch up sides of 8x8-inch ungreased pan.
◊ Stir together 1 cup sugar, 3 tablespoons flour, lemon juice, cinnamon and salt. Add sliced peaches and toss gently to combine. Spoon mixture into crust. Sprinkle reserved crust mixture over peaches.
◊ Bake in 450° oven for 10 minutes. Reduce heat to 350° and continue baking for 40 minutes, or until peaches are tender and crust is lightly browned. Serve warm or cold.
◊ NOTE: May be topped with ice cream or whipped cream.

PEARS

Unlike most fruits, pears are actually better if picked from the tree **before** they are fully ripe. If allowed to ripen on the tree, pears can develop an off flavor and gritty texture. After a few days of ripening, Michigan pears are juicy, sweet and delicious.

MAJOR GROWING AREAS

Fresh Michigan pears are available during the months of August, September and October. Michigan usually ranks 5th or 6th among states producing pears. Many of the pears raised in Michigan are commercially canned.

Cut pears will darken when exposed to the air, so pears must be treated with ascorbic acid or lemon juice before home canning or freezing.

HOW MUCH TO BUY??? 4 medium pears usually weigh a pound and will yield 2 cups sliced pears. Allow 1 pear per serving.

SELECTION: Choose firm (but not hard) unblemished fruit. A ripe pear will yield to gentle pressure. Slight scarring or small blemishes are common and won't affect the quality of the pear.

AVOID: Discard fruit which is bruised, shriveled, or has soft flesh near the stem.

STORAGE: For best flavor, pears are picked before they are fully ripe. To ripen pears, store pears at room temperature away from sunlight, in a loosely closed paper bag or ripening bowl. Fully ripened pears should be refrigerated and used within a week.

PEARS

This pie recipe is a little different from most pie recipes, but it is my favorite kind of recipe - easy and delicious!

EASY PEAR PIE
Yield: 1, 9-inch pie

3 or 4 fresh, ripe pears
1 unbaked 9-inch pie crust
1 cup sugar
1 cup all-purpose flour
1/4 cup melted butter or margarine
2 eggs
1 teaspoon lemon juice
1/2 teaspoon vanilla
1/2 teaspoon ground ginger

◊ Preheat oven to 400° F.
◊ Wash and drain pears. Cut pears lengthwise into halves; remove core and stem ends with paring knife.
◊ Arrange pears cut-side-down in pie shell, with wide ends of pears near outside edge of shell. Set aside.
◊ Beat sugar, flour, melted butter, eggs, lemon juice, vanilla and ginger with electric mixer until smooth and blended. Pour into pear-lined shell.
◊ Bake for 40 to 45 minutes, or until golden brown and top springs back when lightly pressed with finger. Serve warm. Refrigerate any leftovers.

PEAR CRISP
Yield: 6 servings

6 cups sliced fresh pears (about 6 medium)
1/3 cup sugar
1 tablespoon lemon juice
1/2 teaspoon finely grated lemon peel
1 cup quick cooking oats
1/3 cup brown sugar, firmly packed
2 tablespoons all-purpose flour
1/2 teaspoon ground cinnamon
1/2 teaspoon ground ginger
4 tablespoons butter or margarine

◊ Preheat oven to 400° F.
◊ In a large bowl, toss pears with sugar, lemon juice and lemon
  peel. Place pears in a lightly greased 8 x 8-inch baking dish.
◊ Combine oats, brown sugar, flour, cinnamon and ginger. Cut
  in butter with a fork or pastry blender until mixture is crumbly.
  Sprinkle over pears.
◊ Bake for 25 to 30 minutes, or until pears are bubbling and
  topping is crisped. Serve warm.

125

FESTIVE FALL COBBLER
Yield: 6 servings

1/2 cup honey or corn syrup
1/4 cup sugar
1 tablespoon cornstarch
1/4 cup water
1 1/2 cup fresh or frozen cranberries
2 medium pears
1 cup all-purpose flour
1/2 cup sugar
1/4 teaspoon baking soda
1 teaspoon baking powder
1/4 cup butter or margarine
1 egg
1/4 cup milk
1/4 cup chopped pecans
Whipped cream or non-dairy whipped topping

◊ Preheat oven to 400° F.
◊ Combine honey or corn syrup, 1/4 cup sugar, cornstarch and
  water in a saucepan. (If desired, mixture may be heated in
  microwave oven. Place honey mixture in a microwave safe
  bowl.) Stir in cranberries. Heat to a boil; then simmer 5
  minutes, or until cranberries pop. (Or, cook on high power in
  microwave for 4-5 minutes, or until cranberries pop.)
◊ Wash pears, but do not peel. Core and slice pears. Stir into
  cranberry mixture. Pour mixture into a lightly greased 9-inch
  round or square baking pan.
◊ Combine flour, 1/2 cup sugar, baking soda and baking powder.
  Cut in butter until mixture resembles coarse crumbs. Mix egg
  and milk until smooth. Add to flour mixture, stirring until dry
  ingredients are moistened. Gently fold in pecans into dough.
◊ Spoon dough mixture over pears and cranberries in 6 mounds.
  Bake 20 to 25 minutes, or until top is browned and fruit mixture
  is bubbling. Serve with whipped cream, if desired.

BLUSHING POACHED PEARS
Yield: 4 servings

4 medium pears
1 1/2 cups cranberry-apple juice
5 whole cloves
Whipped cream

◊ Peel, halve, and core pears.
◊ Place pears in a medium saucepan and add cranberry-apple juice and cloves. Bring liquid to a boil over medium-high heat.
◊ Lower heat and allow mixture to simmer, uncovered, for 25 to 30 minutes. Baste pears with cooking liquid frequently during cooking.
◊ Pears are done when they are soft. Serve warm or chilled. Garnish each pear with a dollop of whipped cream, if desired.

Ground ginger may be substituted for the fresh ginger in this recipe (use about 1/8 teaspoon), but I won't promise that the flavor will be as good! Fresh ginger is often found in the produce section of the grocery store. It looks like a small twig, but is easily peeled and grated for use in your favorite dishes.

GINGERED PEAR CUPS
Yield: 4 to 6 servings

1 (11 oz.) can mandarin oranges, with liquid
1 teaspoon grated fresh ginger
1 cup seedless, red grapes
3 pears

◊ Place oranges and juice in medium bowl. Stir in ginger.
◊ Cut grapes in half and add to oranges.
◊ Peel and cube pears. Add to other fruits. Cover and chill for a few hours to allow flavors to blend. If desired, divide fruit among individual serving dishes and pour extra juice over fruit.

PEAR DUMPLING DESSERT
Yield: 8 servings

1 1/2 cups sugar, divided
1 1/2 cups water
1 teaspoon ground ginger, divided
1/2 teaspoon ground nutmeg
3 tablespoons butter or margarine
3 pears, peeled and diced
2 cups all-purpose flour
2 teaspoons baking powder
1/2 teaspoon salt
2/3 cup shortening
1/2 cup milk

◊ Preheat oven to 400° F.
◊ Combine 1 1/4 cup sugar, water, 1/2 teaspoon ginger and nutmeg in saucepan. Bring to a boil. Add butter and set syrup aside.
◊ Combine 1/4 cup sugar and 1/2 teaspoon ginger. Stir together with pears.
◊ Sift together flour, baking powder and salt. Cut in shortening until mixture resembles coarse crumbs. Add milk; stir until flour is moistened.
◊ On a lightly floured surface, roll dough into a large rectangle, about 1/8-inch thick. Cut into 8 squares.
◊ Spoon 1/8 of chopped pear mixture onto center of each dough square. Fold corners of each square to center of square and seal edges together. Place in a greased 9 x 13-inch pan.
◊ Pour set aside syrup over dumplings. Bake at 400° for 35 to 40 minutes, or until golden brown. Serve.

PEPPERS

Peppers add zest to salads, soups, sandwiches and stir-fry dishes. Naturally rich in Vitamin C, peppers also supply Vitamin A to our diets (especially the red peppers). As green bell peppers continue to ripen, their color changes from green to bright red. The flavor becomes sweeter as the color turns red. Red bell peppers are mild and sweet, not hot or spicy as some people believe.

MAJOR GROWING AREAS

To prepare fresh peppers for cooking or slicing, start by washing them thoroughly. Next, remove the stem core, seeds and membranes leaving only the pepper shell.

Michigan usually ranks around 7th among states producing peppers. Most peppers raised in Michigan each year are sold as fresh produce.

HOW MUCH TO BUY??? Allow one large pepper per person for stuffed peppers, and 2 to 3 medium peppers to serve 4 people as a side dish.

SELECTION: Buy glossy, firm peppers with few or no blemishes. The sides of the pepper should be thick and firm, not thin or soft. The color may range from bright green to bright red.

AVOID: Peppers with soft, watery spots or other signs of decay should be discarded. Avoid peppers which are withered or show signs of no longer being fresh.

STORAGE: Peppers should be stored in a plastic bag in the crisper drawer in the refrigerator. Fresh peppers will keep for about a week. Peppers which have been cut in pieces should be wrapped in plastic, refrigerated and used as quickly as possible.

129

GREEN PEPPER CASSEROLE
Yield: 4 servings

1/2 cup long grain rice
1 tablespoon butter or margarine
1 green bell pepper, seeded and cut in strips
2 beef flavored bouillon cubes
1 cup boiling water
1 pound ground beef
1/2 cup chopped onion
1/2 cup chopped celery
1 clove garlic, minced
1 (8 oz.) can pizza sauce
1 cup (4 oz.) shredded Cheddar cheese

◊ Preheat oven to 375° F.
◊ Heat rice and butter together in skillet until rice is lightly toasted, stirring frequently. Spread rice in greased 8 x 8-inch pan. Arrange pepper strips on top of rice. Dissolve bouillon in water. Pour over rice. Cover with foil. Bake for 20 minutes.
◊ In skillet, cook beef, onion, celery and garlic until meat is no longer pink, stirring frequently. Drain off excess liquid. Add pizza sauce to meat, cover and simmer for 5 minutes.
◊ Pour meat mixture over peppers and rice. Cover and bake 5 more minutes. Sprinkle with cheese and bake uncovered for 5 minutes. Serve warm.

Make up enough to serve one, two or quite a few! The recipe can easily be multiplied for more sandwiches.

HARVEST MELT SANDWICH
Yield: 1 sandwich

2 slices toasted rye bread
Dijon mustard
1 slice onion
2-3 green pepper slices
1/2 teaspoon butter or margarine
2 thin slices corned beef
1 slice Monterey Jack cheese (or your favorite)
1 tomato slice

◊ Spread bread with mustard, as desired.
◊ Place onion, peppers and margarine in small microwave safe bowl. Cover and cook on high power for 1 to 2 minutes, or until vegetables are tender.
◊ Layer corned beef, pepper mixture and cheese on one bread slice. Place on paper towel and cook on high power in microwave for 20 to 25 seconds, or until cheese just starts to melt. Top with tomato slice and second slice of bread. Serve immediately.

ORANGE CHICKEN WITH PEPPERS
Yield: 4 servings

1/4 cup orange juice
1/2 teaspoon grated orange peel
1 clove garlic, minced
1 tablespoon sugar
1 tablespoon cornstarch
1 tablespoon soy sauce
1/2 teaspoon ground ginger
1/3 cup water
2 whole chicken breasts, boned and skinned
1/4 teaspoon ground black pepper
2 tablespoons vegetable oil
1 medium red bell pepper, seeded and thinly sliced
1 medium green bell pepper, seeded and thinly sliced
Hot, cooked rice

◊ In a small bowl combine orange juice, orange peel, garlic, sugar, cornstarch, soy sauce, ginger and water. Set aside.
◊ Cut chicken into 1-inch cubes. Season with pepper. Heat oil in large skillet or wok. Add chicken and sauté over high heat 3 to 4 minutes, or until chicken is no longer pink. Stir frequently during cooking. Remove chicken from skillet and set aside.
◊ Add bell peppers to skillet. Stir-fry for 2 minutes, or until crisp-tender. Return chicken to skillet and add reserved sauce. Stirring constantly, cook chicken and peppers one minute longer, or until sauce thickens. Serve over hot rice.

GARDEN TWIST PASTA SALAD
Yield: 8 servings

8 ounces rotini (twist) pasta
1 medium green bell pepper
1 cucumber
1 bunch green onions, sliced
1/4 cup sliced black olives
1 tablespoon fresh minced parsley
1/2 cup bottled Italian salad dressing
1 cup cherry tomatoes

◊ Cook pasta according to package directions. Rinse with cold water to cool pasta. Drain thoroughly and set aside.

◊ Remove stem and seeds from pepper , thinly slice and cut into 1 inch long strips. Peel cucumber, cut into fourths lengthwise. Slice cucumbers into 1/4-inch thick slices.

◊ In a large bowl, combine green pepper, cucumber, green onions, olives, parsley and drained pasta. Pour bottled salad dressing over pasta and vegetables. Toss lightly to coat mixture with salad dressing. Cover and refrigerate several hours to allow flavors to blend.

◊ Just before serving, cut tomatoes into fourths. Stir tomatoes into pasta salad.

Suggested Menu

Grilled Hamburgers with Sauteéd Onions
Garden Twist Pasta Salad
Berry and Peach Gelatin Salad
Michigan Cherry Pie

133

This is a favorite during the summer when freshly picked peppers are plentiful. By using the microwave, the kitchen stays cool and so do you!

STUFFED PEPPERS
Yield: 4 servings

4 green bell peppers
3 cups boiling water
1/2 lb. ground beef, cooked and drained
1 bunch (4 to 6) green onions, thinly sliced
1 (14.5 oz.) can stewed tomatoes
1 cup cooked rice
1 teaspoon Worcestershire sauce
1/2 teaspoon salt
1/4 teaspoon chili powder

◊ Cut off tops of each pepper. Remove seeds and inner membrane from each. Place peppers in 2-quart casserole and add boiling water. Cover and cook on high power for 4 to 5 minutes, or until partially cooked. Drain off water.

◊ Combine cooked beef, sliced onions, tomatoes, rice, Worcestershire sauce, salt and chili powder. Place partially cooked peppers in a 9-inch round microwave safe dish. Fill each pepper with beef mixture. Place any leftover beef mixture in the bottom of the dish. Cover loosely with plastic wrap and cook on high power for 8 to 10 minutes, or until filling is heated. Serve warm.

◊ NOTE: Peppers may be prepared and stuffed ahead and refrigerated. Increase cooking time slightly if peppers are refrigerator temperature.

POTATOES

Most of the Michigan potato crop each year is sold for table use or processed into potato chips. According to the Michigan Potato Industry Commission, harvest of potatoes starts in early July in the Bay County area. The first potatoes to be harvested are the "new pota-

MAJOR GROWING AREAS

toes". These potatoes generally come to market directly from the field without being stored. In the fall, harvest of storage potatoes begins in October.

Potatoes are a staple in our diets because of their versatility. Potatoes can be fried, boiled, or baked and they are used in everything from casseroles to stews to salads. Relatively low in calories, potatoes supply Vitamins C and B6 to our diets. It is best to serve potatoes with the skin left on the potato to preserve nutrients. When potatoes must be peeled, don't peel them until the last minute. Peeled potatoes will darken in color if not used quickly.

There is one more unique use for this versatile vegetable. Potatoes can save the day when you add too much salt to soups. Cut a raw potato in half and drop it into the soup. Boil the soup for a short time until excess salt is absorbed. Remove and discard the potato.

HOW MUCH TO BUY??? Allow one medium or large potato per person. With smaller potatoes like new potatoes, 2 pounds will serve 4 or 5 people. There are usually 3 medium potatoes per pound.

SELECTION: Look for potatoes which are well-shaped, firm, even colored, and smooth. The color may range from reddish brown to light brown. The size of potato does not affect the flavor of the potato. When baking potatoes in the microwave, it is important to select potatoes of the same size so they will cook evenly.

AVOID: Discard potatoes with a green tinge to the skin or areas of green "sunburn" on the skin. The flavor of these potatoes will be bitter. Do not select potatoes with large cuts or cracks or potatoes which are

135

shriveled or sprouted.

STORAGE: Do not wash potatoes before storing them. Do not store potatoes in the refrigerator. At refrigerator temperatures, some of the starch in potatoes turns to sugar, making the potato undesirably sweet. Store potatoes in a cool place, preferably at around 50° F. Potatoes should be stored in a dark, dry, well-ventilated area. If potatoes are purchased in a plastic bag, you may wish to transfer them to a net bag so the potatoes stay dry and ventilated. At home, potatoes will store well for 2 to 4 weeks.

RED ONION POTATO SALAD
Yield: 6 servings

6 medium Michigan potatoes, peeled, freshly cooked and sliced
1 cup sliced celery
1 cup red onion, thinly sliced and cut into bite size pieces
1/3 cup chopped parsley
1/4 cup low-calorie Italian dressing
3 tablespoons wine vinegar
2 teaspoons salt
Dash cayenne pepper

◊ Cut potatoes into bite size pieces. In large bowl, combine hot potatoes with celery, onion, and parsley. Stir together Italian dressing, vinegar, salt and pepper. Pour dressing over potatoes and toss lightly until blended. Refrigerate to chill.
◊ TIP: Marinating hot potatoes in dressing while they chill brings out the full flavor - so, you need less dressing!

The Michigan Potato Industry Commission
DeWitt, Michigan

This recipe is very flexible. It can easily be doubled or cut in half when needed. Adjust the cooking times and cooking utensils accordingly. Extra vegetables can easily be added for a change of pace. During harvest time, add sliced zucchini, bell peppers or green onions.

POTATO POTPOURRI
Yield: 4 servings

4 medium potatoes, peeled and sliced
1/2 cup chopped onion
1/2 cup chopped carrots
1/4 cup butter or margarine

MICROWAVE DIRECTIONS:
◊ Combine potatoes, onion and carrots in a 1-quart casserole dish. Cut butter into pieces and dot potato mixture with butter. Cook, covered in microwave on high power for 11 to 13 minutes, or until potatoes are nearly tender. Stir 2 to 3 times during cooking time.
◊ Allow to stand, covered, for 2 to 3 minutes before serving to allow potatoes to finish cooking.
◊ HINT: Small amounts of leftover cooked vegetables such as peas, corn and beans can be added near the end of the cooking time. To reduce calories, water may be substituted for butter or margarine.

GRILLING DIRECTIONS:
◊ Combine potatoes, onion and carrots on a double thickness of foil which is about14-inches long. Cut butter into pieces and dot potato mixture with butter. Cover with additional foil. Roll together all edges to seal potatoes in foil packet.
◊ Grill over medium coals for 20 to 30 minutes on one side. Turn and continue grilling for 10 to 20 minutes, or until potatoes are tender.

CHEESY POTATO CASSEROLE
Yield: 8 servings

8 medium potatoes
4 tablespoons butter or margarine
1 pint half-and-half
1/2 teaspoon garlic salt
1/4 teaspoon black pepper
3 tablespoons grated Parmesan cheese
1 cup (4 oz.) shredded Cheddar cheese

◊ Cook potatoes in skins and refrigerate overnight.
◊ Preheat oven to 350° F. Peel and grate potatoes.
◊ Spread potatoes in the bottom of an ungreased 2-quart
  casserole dish.
◊ Melt margarine. Add half-and-half, garlic salt, and pepper to
  melted margarine. Pour over potatoes.
◊ Sprinkle Parmesan cheese over potatoes. Spread Cheddar
  cheese over Parmesan cheese layer. Bake for 60 minutes, or
  until bubbling.

REFRIGERATOR POTATO ROLLS
Yield: 3 dozen rolls

1 (1/4 oz.) pkg. active dry yeast
1 1/2 cups lukewarm water
1/2 cup sugar
1 teaspoon salt
1/2 cup vegetable oil
2 eggs
1 cup mashed potatoes (instant mashed potatoes may be prepared and used)
7 cups all-purpose flour

◊ Dissolve yeast in lukewarm water in large bowl. Stir in sugar, salt, oil, eggs and mashed potatoes. Beat with electric mixer until combined.

◊ Add 4 cups of flour. Continue beating until smooth. Stir in enough remaining flour so that mixture is easy to handle. Turn out onto lightly floured surface; knead until smooth and elastic (about 10 minutes).

◊ Place in greased bowl; turn greased side up. Cover bowl with plastic wrap and refrigerate. Chill at least 8 hours, but no longer than 3 or 4 days.

◊ Punch down dough. Let rest 5 to 10 minutes. Shape dough as desired*. Let rise until doubled in size (about 30 to 40 minutes).

◊ Bake on greased pan in **preheated 400° F** oven 15 to 25 minutes, or until golden brown. Serve warm.

*HINT: You may wish to try the following shapes for the rolls-
Crescents: Roll 1/3 dough into 10-inch circle. Spread with softened margarine. Cut into 12 wedges. Roll up beginning at wide end. Tuck point of wedge under roll and place on greased cookie sheet.
Dinner rolls: Break off 1/3 dough. Divide into 12 pieces and roll each into a ball. Bake greased cookie sheet. If desired, cut an x across top of each roll with kitchen scissors.

139

Use your own favorite seasoning in this recipe. Instead of Italian seasoning, you may want to try substituting grated Parmesan cheese, garlic salt, basil, paprika or something to compliment the main course for the meal.

POTATO WEDGES
Yield: 4 servings

4 medium Michigan potatoes
1/4 cup butter or margarine
1 teaspoon Italian seasoning
Salt
Pepper

◊ Preheat oven to 450° F.
◊ Cut each potato into 4 lengthwise wedges. Place on ungreased cookie sheet with skin side down.
◊ Melt butter or margarine. Stir in Italian seasoning. Brush potatoes with seasoned butter. Season with salt and pepper, as desired.
◊ Bake at 450° for 30 to 35 minutes, or until potatoes are tender. Arrange on serving platter. If desired, garnish with parsley.

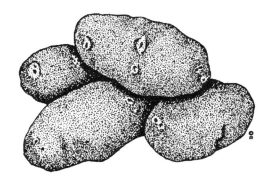

VEGETABLE BEEF SOUP
Yield: 8 servings

1 1/2 pounds stew beef, cut in 1-inch pieces
2 tablespoons vegetable oil
8 cups beef stock or water
1 onion, chopped
2 stalks celery, sliced
2 carrots, peeled and sliced
4 medium potatoes, peeled and cubed
1/4 teaspoon pepper
1 tablespoon salt

◊ Lightly brown stew beef in vegetable oil in large kettle or skillet. Drain off excess fat. Combine stew beef, beef stock, and onion in large kettle. Cover and simmer for 2 hours, or until beef is tender. Skim off excess fat.
◊ Add celery, carrots, potatoes, pepper and salt. Continue to simmer soup for an additional hour, or until vegetables are tender. Serve hot.
◊ HINT: If water is used, you may wish to add 2 beef flavored bouillon cubes for extra flavor.

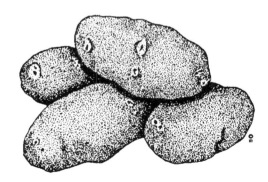

141

AUNT VERA'S FARMER CHOPS
Yield: 6 servings

3 medium potatoes
2 tablespoons vegetable oil
3 cloves garlic, minced
6 pork chops
1 large onion
1 pint dairy sour cream
1 teaspoon ground dry mustard
3/4 teaspoon salt

◊ Slice potatoes in thirds lengthwise. Place in lightly greased 2-quart glass baking dish.
◊ Sauté garlic in oil. Add pork chops and brown lightly on both sides. Arrange chops on top of potatoes in baking dish.
◊ Peel and thinly slice onions. Arrange onion slices over pork chops.
◊ Mix sour cream with dry mustard and salt. Spoon over onions. Bake uncovered in 350° oven for 1 1/2 hours, or until pork chops are thoroughly cooked.

Suggested Menu

Aunt Vera's Farmer Chops
Summer Fruit Salad
Refrigerator Potato Rolls
Heavenly Cherry Angel Food Trifle

THE BEST POTATO SOUP

Yield: 6 servings

3 medium potatoes, peeled and diced
1/4 cup chopped onion
2 cups water
3/4 cup all-purpose flour
3 cups milk
1/4 cup chopped ham
1 tablespoon minced parsley
1/4 teaspoon ground pepper
1/4 teaspoon garlic salt
1 tablespoon butter or margarine

◊ In a medium saucepan, combine potatoes, onion and water. Bring to a boil. Reduce heat and simmer until vegetables are tender.
◊ Stir flour into milk. Add to vegetables and water. Stir in ham, parsley, pepper, garlic salt, and butter.
◊ Let simmer until thickened and creamy. Do not allow mixture to boil.

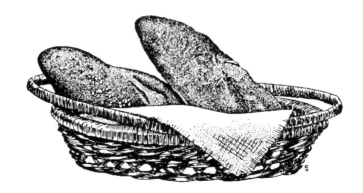

This is a rich casserole which would be great for a luncheon.

BAKED SEAFOOD SALAD
Yield: 6 servings

1 (6.5 oz.) can minced clams, drained
1 (6 oz.) can crab meat, flaked and drained
1 (4.5 oz.) can shrimp, drained
1 cup diced celery
1 green bell pepper, diced
1 cup mayonnaise or salad dressing
1 tablespoon Worcestershire sauce
1 teaspoon lemon juice
Dash hot pepper sauce
1 cup crushed potato chips

◊ Preheat oven to 350° F.
◊ Stir together clams, crab meat, shrimp, celery, and green pepper.
◊ In a small bowl, stir together mayonnaise, Worcestershire sauce, lemon juice and pepper sauce. Fold into seafood mixture.
◊ Spoon seafood mixture into a lightly greased 1 1/2-quart casserole dish. Sprinkle crushed potato chips over casserole. Bake at 350° for 40 to 45 minutes, or until bubbling and heated through.

Suggested Menu

Baked Seafood Salad
Hard Rolls
Tossed Salad
Melon Boats

PURPLE PLUMS

MAJOR GROWING AREAS

Although a variety of plums are raised in the state, most of the plums raised in Michigan are Italian purple plums. The two common Michigan varieties, Stanley and Blufre, have a dark blue-black color with a greenish-yellow flesh. The Blufre plum is a little bigger than the Stanley. The nice thing about both of these plum varieties is that the flesh separates easily from the pit when they are ripe. This makes them much easier to slice or prepare for canning and freezing.

The Italian plum has a higher sugar content than other plums which makes it great for out-of-hand eating. Plums contain no fat, are still relatively low in calories, and supply Vitamin A, Vitamin C and calcium to the diet. Plums also have a high fiber content. Plums can be used in a variety of recipes and may be canned or frozen in a syrup or sugar pack.

Plums are harvested in Michigan from late August through early October. According to the Michigan Plum Advisory Board, Michigan typically ranks around 3rd in the nation in purple plum production with about 500 farms in the state growing plums.

HOW MUCH TO BUY??? There are usually 6 to 8 medium plums per pound.

SELECTION: Choose mature purple plums which are plump, fresh looking, and have a dark blue-black color. Mature plums may need a few days to fully ripen. When ripe, plums will yield to slight pressure from the palm of your hand.

AVOID: Plums which are picked before they are mature will never ripen properly. Immature plums are hard and have poor color. Avoid overripe or very soft plums as well as those showing signs of decay.

STORAGE: Do not wash purple plums until just before using them.

145

PURPLE PLUMS

Ripe plums should be stored in the refrigerator. Use ripe plums within a week. The Michigan Plum Advisory Board notes that plums are juiciest when served at room temperature.

To ripen purple plums, store them for 1 to 2 days at room temperature away from direct sunlight. To speed ripening, store plums in a loosely closed paper bag. The ethylene gas naturally released by the plums will speed up the ripening process.

SPICED PLUM BREAD
Yield: 1 loaf

1 egg
1/2 cup honey
2/3 cup sugar
1 teaspoon vanilla extract
1 teaspoon baking soda
2 cups all-purpose flour
1/4 teaspoon ground cloves
1/8 teaspoon ground cinnamon
1 (1 lb.) can Michigan Plums, drained, pitted, cut into pieces
1 cup chopped walnuts

◊ Preheat oven to 350° F.
◊ In a mixing bowl, beat together egg, honey, sugar and vanilla. Add soda, flour, cloves and cinnamon. Mix until blended. Stir in plum pieces and nuts. DO NOT overmix. Grease and flour one 9 x 5-inch loaf pan. Spread batter in prepared pan.
◊ Bake in 350° oven for 50 to 60 minutes, or until top springs back when lightly touched. If top becomes too brown, cover loosely with foil to prevent overbrowning. Remove from loaf pan and allow to cool on baking rack.
◊ NOTE: Plums can be cut easily with kitchen shears.

Michigan Plum Advisory Board
Lansing, Michigan

This recipe features a purple plum filling in a cookie crust.

PURPLE PLUM TART
Yield: 8 servings

1/2 cup butter or margarine, softened
1 1/2 cups all-purpose flour
1/3 cup sugar
1/4 teaspoon nutmeg
1 (1 lb.) can purple plums, with liquid
1/4 teaspoon almond extract
1 tablespoon cornstarch
Sweetened whipped cream or non-dairy whipped topping
  (optional)

◊ Preheat oven to 375° F.
◊ Combine butter, flour, sugar and nutmeg with pastry blender until mixture is consistency of coarse crumbs. Press mixture evenly into bottom and side of 9-inch springform pan or pie plate.
◊ Set aside juice from canned plums. Pit plums and chop into fine pieces. Combine reserved juice, almond extract and cornstarch. Stir until cornstarch is blended into liquid. Stir in chopped plums. Pour mixture over crust.
◊ Bake at 375° for 50 to 60 minutes, or until pastry is golden. Cool. Cut into wedges, top with whipped cream, if desired.

FRESH AND FRUITY PIZZA
Yield: 10 to 12 servings

1 (20 oz.) pkg. refrigerated sugar cookie dough
2 (8 oz. each) cartons vanilla yogurt
2 eggs, lightly beaten
1/4 cup all-purpose flour
1/2 teaspoon grated orange peel
3 to 4 purple plums, pitted and sliced
1 cup blueberries
1 cup strawberries, hulled and halved
1/4 cup sugar
2 tablespoons cornstarch
2/3 cup water
1/3 cup orange juice

◊ Preheat oven to 400° F.
◊ Grease a 10-inch pizza pan. Slice cookie dough into 1/2-inch
   thick slices and line pizza pan. Flour hands and press cookie
   dough together in pan, forming a crust. Bake at 400° for 10
   minutes. Remove from oven, but leave oven on.
◊ Mix together yogurt, eggs, flour and orange peel in medium
   bowl and spread on crust. Return to oven and bake 10-15
   minutes longer or until filling is barely set. Cool completely.
◊ Arrange plum slices around outer edge of crust. Form a ring of
   blueberries next to plums. Fill center circle with strawberry
   halves.
◊ Combine sugar and cornstarch in a small pan. Add water and
   stir gently over medium heat until mixture boils and thickens.
   Remove from heat and stir in orange juice. Brush glaze over
   fruit. Chill before serving.

PERFECT PLUM CAKE
Yield: 12 servings

3/4 cup shortening
1/2 cup sugar
2 eggs
1 teaspoon vanilla
1 (30 oz.) can purple plums, with liquid
2 cups all-purpose flour
2 teaspoons baking soda
1/2 teaspoon salt
1 cup chopped walnuts or pecans

◊ Preheat oven to 350° F. Grease a bundt pan or tube dish.
◊ Cream together shortening and sugar. Add eggs and vanilla and beat until creamy.
◊ Drain plums, reserving 1 cup of liquid. Pit and chop plums. Add to plum juice. Set aside.
◊ Stir together flour, soda and salt. Beat flour mixture into creamed mixture alternately with plums and juice. Stir in nuts. Pour into prepared pan.
◊ Bake at 350° for 50 to 55 minutes, or until top springs back when lightly pressed with finger. Cool 10 minutes. Remove from pan.
◊ NOTE: Cake may be frosted, glazed or topped with a dollop of sweetened whipped cream.

149

Set aside the barbeque sauce and try plum sauce the next time you grill. You won't be disappointed! The orange adds just the right tang to this sweet sauce featuring plums.

PLUM GLAZED SPARERIBS
Yield: 4 servings

3-4 lbs. spareribs (pork or beef)
1/2 teaspoon salt
1 teaspoon peppercorns
1 onion, peeled and quartered
2 1/2 cups Michigan Plums, fresh, pitted and chopped
1 1/2 cups sugar
1/2 cup orange juice
1 teaspoon orange zest (grated orange peel, without bitter white skin)
3 tablespoons soy sauce
1 tablespoon honey
2 tablespoons dry sherry

◊ Cut ribs into serving size pieces. Place in large dutch oven. Cover ribs with water. Add 1/2 teaspoon salt, 1 teaspoon peppercorns and onion. Bring to boil, cover, and simmer 30 minutes.
◊ While ribs are cooking, prepare plum glaze. Place remaining ingredients in saucepan and simmer slowly until thickened to sauce consistency.
◊ Remove partially cooked ribs from water. Drain and place on grill. Grill until ribs are done, turning frequently. During last 15 minutes of cooking, baste ribs with plum sauce.

Michigan Plum Advisory Board
Lansing, Michigan

STRAWBERRIES

June and July are Michigan strawberry months. The harvest begins in
the southern portion of the state in
early June and moves north to the
Upper Peninsula in July. About 80%
of the crop is used for fresh market
sales. "Pick-your-own" strawberry
patches are popular throughout the
state, but already picked strawber-

MAJOR GROWING AREAS

ries can easily be found in the grocery stores and fruit markets. Michigan typically ranks around 5th or 6th in strawberry production in the
United States.

Ripe, red, firm strawberries are delicious and good for you too! With
less than 60 calories per cup, strawberries are high in vitamin C. One
cup of strawberries supplies about 150% of the U. S. Recommended
Daily Allowance for Vitamin C. In addition, strawberries provide some
iron to our diet, are low in sodium and contain no fat!

Whole strawberries can be dipped in powdered sugar, chocolate fondue
or dipped in plain yogurt followed by a second dip in brown sugar. Of
course, it wouldn't be summer without at least one strawberry pie.
Purée strawberries for a fresh strawberry sauce (sweeten if desired) and
serve over other fruits, ice cream or cakes. Puréed strawberries will
freeze well as is, or sweetened with a small amount of sugar.

HOW MUCH TO BUY??? 1 pint of strawberries usually serves 2 people.
On the average, one pint of strawberries weighs about 3/4 of a pound
and will yield a little more than 2 cups of sliced berries.

SELECTION: Look for strawberries with a full, red color. Strawberries
will not ripen after being picked. The flesh of the fruit should be firm and
well rounded. The bright green stem cap (or hull) should still be
attached.

AVOID: Stay away from berries with large uncolored areas, a dull
shrunken appearance and strawberries with large seedy areas. Strawberries which are soft should be avoided as this may be a sign of
overripeness or decay. Mold can spread quickly from one berry to the

next, so moldy and overripe berries should be discarded.

STORAGE: Place strawberries in the refrigerator immediately. Do not wash strawberries until just before using them. To wash berries, rinse gently with a spray of cool water. Do not allow berries to soak in the water, or they will become mushy. The stem caps protect the berry and should not be removed until just before using the berry. Strawberries will keep for a few days in the refrigerator, but should be used as quickly as possible for best flavor and highest nutritional value.

What could be better than strawberry pie in early summer? The cream cheese layer makes this pie especially good.

FRESH MEYER STRAWBERRY FARM PIE
Yield: 1, 9-inch pie

1 1/4 cup sugar
1 1/4 cup water
3 tablespoons cornstarch
Pinch salt
1 tablespoon lemon juice
1 (3 oz.) pkg. strawberry flavored gelatin
1 9-inch pie crust, cooked and cooled
1 (3 oz.) pkg. softened cream cheese (optional)
4 cups strawberries, hulled and sliced
Whipped cream or non-dairy whipped topping

◊ Combine sugar, water, cornstarch, salt and lemon juice in saucepan. Boil until clear. Add strawberry gelatin and stir until dissolved. Cool slightly.
◊ If desired, spread softened cream cheese on bottom of prepared pie shell. Spread sliced strawberries over pie shell. Pour gelatin mixture over strawberries in pie shell. Chill until firm.
◊ Garnish each serving with whipped cream or non-dairy topping, as desired.

Barb Meyer
Meyer Berry Farm
Northville, Michigan

STRAWBERRY ICE CREAM
Yield: 1 gallon

3 large eggs
1 cup sugar
1/2 teaspoon salt
1/8 teaspoon ground cinnamon
5 cups milk
1 (13 oz.) can evaporated milk
1 (14 oz.) can sweetened condensed milk
1 tablespoon vanilla
**1 pint crushed strawberries sweetened with 4 tablespoons
  sugar**

◊ Beat eggs in large mixing bowl. Add 1 cup sugar, salt and
  cinnamon, beating until completely blended.
◊ Bring 5 cups milk to a boil, stirring often.
◊ Add small amount of hot milk to egg mixture, stirring con-
  stantly. Gradually add remaining hot milk, stirring constantly.
  Add evaporated milk, sweetened condensed milk and vanilla.
  Stir in crushed strawberries and juice. Chill mixture in refrigera-
  tor or freezer.
◊ Pour into a 4 quart ice cream container. Freeze according to
  freezer directions.

153

OVERNIGHT STRAWBERRY DANISH ROLLS
Yield: 24 rolls

2 (1/4 oz. each) pkgs. active dry yeast
1 teaspoon sugar
1/2 cup lukewarm water
4 cups all-purpose flour
1/3 cup sugar
1/2 teaspoon salt
1 cup (2 sticks) butter or margarine
1 cup milk
4 egg yolks
1 egg white, slightly beaten
1 (10 oz.) jar strawberry jam
Glaze:
1 tablespoon milk (or more if needed)
1 cup powdered sugar

◊ Combine yeast, 1 teaspoon sugar and water in medium size bowl. Let stand 5 minutes.
◊ Stir together flour, 1/3 cup sugar and salt. Cut in butter until mixture resembles cornmeal. Add milk, beaten egg yolks, and softened yeast. Mix with wooden spoon to make soft dough. Cover with plastic wrap and refrigerate 8 to 24 hours.
◊ When ready to bake, punch down dough. Let dough rest for 5 to 10 minutes. Divide dough into 4 equal balls. Cut each ball into 6 pieces (to make 24 rolls). Using lightly floured hands and a lightly floured board, roll each piece of dough into a 10-inch rope. Coil each rope loosely on a greased baking sheet, tucking under the ends to form rolls. Brush with beaten egg white (place extra egg white in refrigerator for later use) and let rise 25 minutes, or until almost doubled.
◊ Make a deep indentation in center of each roll. Fill with jam and brush with beaten egg white again. Bake in **preheated 350° F** oven for 15 to 20 minutes, or until golden.
◊ Stir together milk and powdered sugar to make a glaze. Drizzle over warm rolls.

Because this recipe uses frozen strawberries, it can be enjoyed throughout the year. Don't forget to add the pecans! They make this bread taste especially good.

STRAWBERRY-PECAN BREAD

Yield: 1 loaf

2 eggs
1 cup sugar
1/4 cup vegetable oil
1 (10 oz.) pkg. frozen, sliced strawberries in syrup, partially thawed
1 3/4 cups all-purpose flour
1 teaspoon ground cinnamon
1/2 teaspoon baking soda
1/2 teaspoon salt
1 cup chopped pecans

◊ Preheat oven to 375° F.
◊ Beat eggs in large mixing bowl. Add sugar and oil. Beat until well-mixed. Add partially thawed strawberries and beat until no large chunks of strawberries remain.
◊ Stir together flour, cinnamon, baking soda and salt. Stir into strawberry mixture. Add the pecans and stir until just combined.
◊ Pour into greased 9 x 5-inch loaf pan. Bake in 375° oven for 55 to 65 minutes, or until a toothpick inserted near center comes out clean.
◊ Cool in the pan for 5 to 10 minutes. Remove from pan and cool on wire rack.

STRAWBERRY SHORTCAKES
Yield: 4 servings

1 quart of strawberries, hulled and sliced
1/2 cup sugar
2 cups all-purpose flour
3 teaspoons baking powder
1 tablespoon sugar
1/2 teaspoon salt
1/2 cup butter or margarine
3/4 cup milk
1 cup whipping cream
2 tablespoons sugar
1 teaspoon vanilla

◊ Preheat oven to 450° F. Sprinkle sliced strawberries with 1/2 cup sugar; set aside.

◊ Sift together flour, baking powder, 1 tablespoon sugar and salt in a large bowl. Cut in butter until mixture resembles rice. Add milk and stir until blended. Knead dough briefly on a lightly floured surface and roll out dough until 1/2-inch thick. Cut into shortcakes with a floured 3 to 3 1/2-inch biscuit cutter. Place on ungreased cookie sheet. Bake 15 to 18 minutes, or until golden brown.

◊ Beat together chilled whipping cream, 2 tablespoons sugar and vanilla in a small bowl until stiff peaks form.

◊ Split each shortcake crosswise, mound with berries, top with other half of shortcake, mound with berries and top with a dollop of whipped cream.

SUGAR BEETS

MAJOR GROWING AREAS

Well over 100,000 acres of sugar beets are planted in Michigan each year. Most of the sugar beets are grown in the Saginaw Valley and Thumb growing areas where the rich, flat land is most suitable for sugar beet growth. In a typical year, the 55 million pounds of sugar produced in the state make Michigan this country's 5th leading producer of beet sugar.

A mature sugar beet weighs 3 to 5 pounds and is about one foot in length. Harvest starts in late September and continues through November. The beets are stored outside before being processed and are kept cool naturally by cooler fall air temperatures. The storage piles are 20 feet high, 120 feet wide and can be up to one-quarter mile in length. Beets are removed from the storage piles over the next few months and on into early winter months as they are processed into granulated sugar. Processing plants are usually located near the growing areas.

One beet is processed into about 5 ounces of pure beet sugar, along with some by-products such as molasses and beet pulp.

STORAGE: At home, granulated sugar and powdered sugar should be stored in air-tight containers to keep out moisture and prevent caking or lumping. Naturally moist brown sugar can be stored in tightly closed, heavy, moisture-proof plastic bags or in a tightly closed rust-proof container.

157

BLACK BOTTOM CUPS
Yield: 2 dozen cupcakes

Cake:
1 1/2 cups sifted all-purpose flour
1 cup Pioneer sugar
1/4 cup cocoa
1 teaspoon baking soda
1/2 teaspoon salt
1 cup water
1 tablespoon vinegar
1/3 cup vegetable oil
1 teaspoon vanilla

Topping:
1 (8 oz.) pkg. cream cheese
1 egg, beaten
1/3 cup Pioneer sugar
1/8 teaspoon salt
1 (6 oz.) pkg. semisweet chocolate chips

◊ Preheat oven to 350° F.
◊ Cake: Sift together flour, sugar, cocoa, soda, and salt. Add water, vinegar, oil, and vanilla. Beat until well mixed. Fill paper muffin cups 1/3 full with chocolate batter.
◊ Topping: Cream together cream cheese, egg, sugar and salt. Stir in chocolate chips. Top each muffin cup with a heaping teaspoon of the cream cheese mixture. Sprinkle each with additional sugar and chopped pecans, if desired. Bake in 350° oven for 30 to 35 minutes, or until toothpick inserted in cake comes out clean.
◊ Note: Convenient for picnics.

Pioneer Sugar
Michigan Sugar Company
Saginaw, Michigan

PUMPKIN COOKIES
Yield: 3 1/2 dozen cookies

1 cup shortening
1/2 cup Big Chief Brown Sugar, firmly packed
1/2 cup Big Chief Granulated Sugar
1 cup pumpkin
1 egg
1 teaspoon vanilla
1 teaspoon baking soda
2 cups all-purpose flour
1 teaspoon baking powder
1 teaspoon ground cinnamon
1/2 teaspoon salt
1 cup chopped nuts (optional)

◊ Preheat oven to 350° F.
◊ Cream together shortening, Big Chief Brown Sugar, and Big Chief Granulated Sugar. Beat in pumpkin, egg and vanilla.
◊ Mix together soda, flour, baking powder, cinnamon and salt and add to creamed mixture. Stir in nuts. Drop by spoonful onto greased cookie sheet. Bake 10 to 12 minutes. Cool.

Big Chief Sugar
Monitor Sugar Company
Bay City, Michigan

PEANUT BRITTLE
Yield: about 50 pieces

2 cups Pioneer sugar
1/2 cup light corn syrup
1/4 cup boiling water
2 cups raw peanuts
1 teaspoon baking soda

◊ Bring to a boil the sugar, corn syrup, water and peanuts in a large iron pot. Cook for about 20 minutes, or until mixture reaches 290° F. Stir frequently during cooking. Remove from heat. Stir in soda (do not beat mixture).
◊ Pour at once into a large buttered pan. Break into pieces when cool.

Pioneer Sugar
Michigan Sugar Company
Saginaw, Michigan

Your local market will have plenty of fresh Michigan produce available during the summer months. Look for the foods listed by each month during all or at least part of that month.

◊ During **July** look for: *green beans, green bell peppers, cherries, celery, cucumbers, carrots, blueberries, potatoes, sweet corn, peaches, and apples.*
◊ During **August** look for: *cherries, green beans, green bell peppers, celery, carrots, sweet corn, cucumbers, cantaloupe, potatoes, tomatoes, apples, blueberries, pears, and peaches.*
◊ During **September** look for: *green beans, green bell peppers, celery, carrots, sweet corn, cucumbers, cantaloupe, potatoes, tomatoes, apples, blueberries, onions, plums, pears, blueberries, and peaches.*

BLACKBERRY CAKE
Yield: 12 servings

1 quart blackberries
3/4 cup sugar
3 cups marshmallows (about 20 large marshmallows)
1 (3 oz.) pkg. berry flavored gelatin mix
1 (18.5 oz.) yellow or white cake mix, prepared according to
  package directions, but unbaked
Ice cream or sweetened, whipped cream (optional)

◊ Preheat oven to 350° F.
◊ Pour berries into buttered 9 x 13-inch pan. Sprinkle sugar, marshmallows and gelatin mix over berries.
◊ Pour prepared cake batter evenly over berries and marshmallows. Bake at 350° for 50 to 55 minutes, or until top is browned and a toothpick inserted near center comes out clean.
◊ Cool. Invert cake when serving so berries are on top of each slice of cake. If desired, top with ice cream or sweetened, whipped cream.

Martha Schaub
Manitou Market and Bakery
Lake Leelanau, Michigan

Suggested Menu

Plum Glazed Spareribs
Red Onion Potato Salad
Almond Asparagus
Blackberry Cake

161

PUDDING SURPRISE
Yield: 6 to 8 servings

1 cup all-purpose flour
3/4 cup Big Chief granulated sugar
2 tablespoons cocoa
2 teaspoons baking powder
1/2 teaspoon salt
1/2 cup milk
2 tablespoons salad oil
1 teaspoon vanilla
3/4 cup chopped walnuts
3/4 cup Big Chief brown sugar
1/4 cup cocoa
1-3/4 cup hot water

◊ Preheat oven to 350° F.
◊ Mix together flour, Big Chief granulated sugar, cocoa, baking
  powder and salt. Add milk, oil and vanilla and mix well. Batter
  will be stiff. Pour into greased 8x8x2-inch pan.
◊ Combine walnuts, Big Chief Brown Sugar, cocoa and water.
  Mixture will be watery. Pour over batter. Bake 45 minutes.
  Center will be wet. Cool.

Big Chief Sugar
Monitor Sugar Company
Bay City, Michigan

TOMATOES

Tomatoes are plentiful at vegetable stands and in home gardens across the state during the months of August and September. Many of Michigan's tomatoes are processed and the others are sold as fresh produce.

MAJOR GROWING AREAS

Whether or not to peel tomatoes before slicing is an individual choice. When you do need to peel a tomato, try this: Drop the tomato in scalding water for about 30 seconds and then carefully remove the tomato from the water with tongs or a big spoon. The tomato may be peeled as soon as it is cool enough to handle. Tomatoes may be slice two ways. For sandwiches, slice off the stem and blossom ends. Cut thin slices off the remaining tomato. For eating as a side dish, make tomato wedges by slicing from the stem end to the blossom (similar to slicing an apple). Slicing the tomato into wedges will help keep the juice and seeds intact.

One more hint regarding tomatoes. If you buy tomatoes from the store during the winter, place them in a paper sack and store them at room temperature for a few days. The color and flavor will be much improved.

HOW MUCH TO BUY??? In one pound, there are typically 3 medium tomatoes. One pound will serve 3 to 4 and equals 1 1/2 cups peeled and seeded tomatoes.

SELECTION: Choose tomatoes which are well-formed, smooth and that have a good tomato fragrance. Tomatoes which have been ripened with ethylene gas will not have the same "tomato smell" as vine-ripened tomatoes. A ripe tomato will have an rich red-orange color and will yield to light pressure from your finger.

AVOID: Tomatoes which have large areas of green or yellow near the stem should be avoided. Soft, overripe tomatoes should be discarded. Tomatoes with blemishes, bruises, soft spots or slits in the peel should also be avoided.

163

TOMATOES

STORAGE: To ripen tomatoes at home, keep tomatoes at room temperature, away from direct sunlight, standing on the stem end until they are deeply colored and ripe. Tomatoes should be washed just before they are to be used. Ripe tomatoes may be stored in the refrigerator. Some people feel that chilled tomatoes are not as flavorful as room temperature tomatoes. This is a matter of personal preference. Tomatoes will store well in the refrigerator for about a week. Be careful to store them in a single layer to avoid bruising the tomatoes.

PEG'S PICANTE SAUCE
Yield: 6 pints sauce

8 cups peeled, cored, and chopped tomatoes
3 green bell peppers, chopped
2 medium onions, chopped
4 jalapeño peppers, chopped
3 cloves garlic, minced
1 cup vinegar
2 tablespoons salt
2 tablespoons sugar
3/4 teaspoon ground oregano
3/4 teaspoon ground red cayenne pepper
3/4 teaspoon ground cumin

◊ Place tomatoes, bell peppers, onions, jalapeño peppers, and garlic in a large saucepan. Stir in vinegar, salt and sugar.
◊ Simmer, uncovered for 30 to 40 minutes, or until desired consistency.
◊ Stir in oregano, cayenne pepper and cumin. Pour into hot, sterilized jars, leaving 1/2-inch headspace. Adjust lids. Process by boiling water-bath method for 15 minutes.
◊ HINT: Instead of chopping by hand, the vegetables may be processed in food processor until pieces are the size you like.
◊ HINT: You may want to wear clean plastic gloves when cutting jalapeño or other hot peppers to protect your hands.

164

FRESH TOMATO SOUP
Yield: 6 servings

2 tablespoons butter or margarine
1/4 cup chopped onion
1/4 cup chopped celery
2 cloves garlic, minced
2 to 3 pounds fresh tomatoes (or enough to make 3 1/2 cups purée)
2 (13 3/4 oz. each) cans chicken broth
1/4 cup finely chopped parsley
1 teaspoon dried basil

◊ In a medium stockpot or saucepan, melt butter over medium heat. Sauté onion, celery and garlic in butter until tender.
◊ Peel tomatoes and cut into large pieces. Process tomatoes in blender or food processor until puréed. Add 3 1/2 cups tomato purée, chicken broth, parsley and basil to onion mixture. Bring mixture to a boil. Reduce heat and simmer 45 minutes. Chill or serve warm.
◊ NOTE: If desired, soup may be processed in blender or food processor before heating so that other vegetables and seasonings are also puréed.

SPAGHETTI SAUCE
Yield: 4 servings

1/2 lb. ground beef
1 small onion, chopped
1/2 green pepper, chopped
1 clove garlic, chopped
1 (15 oz.) can tomato sauce
1 tablespoon Worcestershire sauce
1 tablespoon sugar
1 teaspoon basil
1/2 teaspoon salt
1/4 teaspoon pepper
Hot, cooked spaghetti

◊ Place ground beef, onion, green pepper and garlic in a large
  skillet. Cook together until meat is no longer pink and vegetables are tender, stirring frequently. Drain off fat.
◊ Add tomato sauce, Worcestershire sauce, sugar, basil, salt,
  and pepper to meat mixture. Simmer tomato mixture until
  flavors are blended and sauce is hot.
◊ Serve over hot, cooked spaghetti.

P·A·S·T·A

FESTIVE RICE
Yield: 8 servings

2 cups long grain rice
3 tablespoons vegetable oil
1 medium onion, chopped
1 bell pepper, chopped
1/3 cup diced celery
1 (16 oz.) can stewed tomatoes, with liquid
1/4 teaspoon ground black pepper

◊ Cook rice according to package instructions.
◊ Preheat oven to 350° F.
◊ Heat oil in a skillet. Add onion, pepper and celery. Sauté vegetables until tender, stirring frequently.
◊ Stir together cooked rice, sautéed vegetables, stewed tomatoes, and pepper. Spoon into a lightly greased 2-quart casserole dish. Bake, covered, at 350° for 15 to 20 minutes, or until heated through.
◊ NOTE: Rice and vegetables may also be cooked, covered, in the microwave oven on high power for 4 to 6 minutes, or until heated through.

TOMATO RELISH
Yield: 3 - 4 cups relish

4 fresh tomatoes
1 medium onion, chopped
1 green bell pepper, chopped
1/2 cup chopped celery
1/2 cup vinegar
1 tablespoon sugar
1 teaspoon salt

◊ Chop tomatoes and drain off excess juice. Combine tomatoes, onion, pepper and celery.
◊ In a small bowl, stir together vinegar, sugar and salt. Pour vinegar mixture over tomatoes. Stir lightly. Chill and serve.

INDEX

INDEX

170

GRAPES AND WINE (cont.)
  The Natural Warmer, 87
GREEN BEAN-TOMATO
  SAUTÉ, 91
GREEN BEANS, 89-92
  Green Bean-Tomato Sauté, 91
  Fresh Green Bean Salad, 90
  Microwave Green Beans with
    Pepper Butter, 92
  Saucy Green Beans, 90
  Savory Green Beans and
    Potatoes, 92
GREEN PEPPER
  CASSEROLE, 130
GREEN PEPPERS, see PEPPERS
HAM AND BEAN BAKE, 80
HARVEST MELT SANDWICH, 131
HEAVENLY CHERRY ANGEL
  FOOD TRIFLE, 62
HONEY, 93-98
  Cornmeal Muffins, 98
  Fruit Kebabs, 38
  Honey and Mustard Glazed
    Chicken, 96
  Honey Butter, 96
  Honey Oatmeal Bread, 94
  Honey Pumpkin Pie, 95
  Peanut Butter and Honey
    Cookies, 97
  Spiced Plum Bread, 146
HONEY AND MUSTARD GLAZED
  CHICKEN, 96
HONEY BUTTER, 96
HONEY OATMEAL BREAD, 94
HONEY PUMPKIN PIE, 95
IRRESISTIBLE M & M CORN
  CRUNCH, 70
LATTICE-TOPPED BLUEBERRY
  PIE, 30
LAYERED ASPARAGUS
  SUPREME, 24
LEMON BROILED SCALLOPS
  AND MUSHROOMS, 108
LEMON GLAZED BLUEBERRY
  TURNOVERS, 34
LIME-POPPY SEED DRESSING
  FOR FRUIT SALADS, 36

MAIN DISHES
  Asparagus and Chicken
    Stir-Fry, 23
  Asparagus Brunch Bundles, 26
  Aunt Vera's Farmer Chops, 142
  Baked Seafood Salad, 144
  Broiled Chicken "Little Traverse
    Bay", 63
  Cherried Pork Chops, 60
  Chicken and Carrot
    Casserole, 40
  Fenn Valley Grilled or Baked
    Cod, 86
  Green Pepper Casserole, 130
  Ham and Bean Bake, 80
  Honey and Mustard Glazed
    Chicken, 96
  Lemon Broiled Scallops and
    Mushrooms, 108
  Miss Lizzie's Tasty Tuna
    Salad, 74
  Orange Chicken with
    Peppers, 132
  Plum Glazed Spareribs, 150
  Pork Chow Mein, 47
  Saturday Night Supper, 78
  Spaghetti Sauce, 166
  Stuffed Peppers, 134
  "Tex-Mex" Style Pot Roast, 82
MAKE AHEAD MICHIGAN
  SALAD, 73
MAPLE APPLESAUCE
  MUFFINS, 103
MAPLE FLAVORED
  FROSTING, 104
MAPLE PECAN SQUARES, 100
MAPLE SYRUP, 99-104
  Maple Applesauce Muffins, 103
  Maple Flavored Frosting, 104
  Maple Pecan Squares, 100
  Maple Syrup Dressing, 102
  Microwaved Maple Squash, 101
MAPLE SYRUP DRESSING, 102
MARINATED MUSHROOMS, 107
MAY WINE SLUSH, 88
MEATS, see Main Dishes
MELON BOATS, 37

171

INDEX

MELONS, see CANTALOUPE
MICHIGAN CHERRY PIE, 64
MICHIGAN MORNING SOUP, 54
MICROWAVE GREEN BEANS
  WITH PEPPER BUTTER, 92
MICROWAVED MAPLE
  SQUASH, 101
MISS IDA'S DILLED POTATO
  SALAD, 76
MISS LIZZIE'S TASTY TUNA
  SALAD, 74
MUSHROOM SAUCE, 106
MUSHROOMS, 105-110
  Lemon Broiled Scallops and
    Mushrooms, 108
  Marinated Mushrooms, 107
  Mushroom Sauce, 106
  Onion Paté, 115
  Phillips Mill Marvelous Morel
    Sundae, 109
  Pork Chow Mein, 47
  Simply Delicious Mushroom
    Appetizers, 110
ONION PÂTÉ, 115
ONION SOUP, 114
ONIONS, 111-116
  Aunt Vera's Farmer Chops, 142
  Cheesy Vegetable Soup, 116
  Chili Bean Soup, 79
  City Slicker Beans, 81
  Festive Rice, 167
  Green Pepper Casserole, 130
  Onion Paté, 115
  Onion Soup, 114
  Red Onion Potato Salad, 136
  Rice-Onion-Cheese
    Casserole, 113
  Sautéed Onions for
    Hamburgers, 112
  Spaghetti Sauce, 166
  Tomato Relish, 167
ORANGE CHICKEN WITH
  PEPPERS, 132
OVERNIGHT STRAWBERRY
  DANISH ROLLS, 154
PEACH ALEXANDER, 88
PEACH CRUMBLE, 122

PEACH MUFFINS, 120
PEACH POPS, 119
PEACHES, 117-122
  Berry and Peach Gelatin
    Salad, 119
  Chiffon Peach Pie, 121
  Michigan Morning Soup, 54
  Peach Alexander, 88
  Peach Crumble, 122
  Peach Muffins, 120
  Peach Pops, 119
  Peaches and Cream
    Cheesecake, 118
PEACHES AND CREAM
  CHEESECAKE, 118
PEANUT BRITTLE, 160
PEANUT BUTTER AND HONEY
  COOKIES, 97
PEAR CRISP, 125
PEAR DUMPLING DESSERT, 128
PEARS, 123-128
  Blushing Poached Pears, 127
  Easy Pear Pie, 124
  Festive Fall Cobbler, 126
  Gingered Pear Cups, 127
  Michigan Morning Soup, 54
  Pear Crisp, 125
  Pear Dumpling Dessert, 128
PEG'S PICANTE SAUCE, 164
PEPPERS, 129-134
  Baked Seafood Salad, 144
  Chili Bean Soup, 79
  Festive Rice, 167
  Garden Twist Pasta Salad, 133
  Green Pepper Casserole, 130
  Harvest Melt Sandwich, 131
  Orange Chicken with
    Peppers, 132
  Pickled Carrots, 44
  Spaghetti Sauce, 166
  Stuffed Peppers, 134
  Tomato Relish, 167
PERFECT PARTY
  TRIANGLES, 75
PERFECT PLUM CAKE, 149
PHILLIPS MILL MARVELOUS
  MOREL SUNDAE, 109

172

INDEX

NOTES